A POCKET GUIDE TO . . .

Atheism

Understanding the inherent problems of a no-God worldview

... GIOUS AGENDA • EVOLUTIONARY
... WORLDVIEW • THE TACTICS OF
... AR RESPONSE TO MORALITY •
... RMER ATHEIS...

A POCKET GUIDE TO . . .

Atheism

Understanding the inherent problems of a no-God worldview

Petersburg, Kentucky, USA

Reprinted January 2017

ISBN: 978-1-60092-976-2

Printed in China.

AnswersInGenesis.org

Table of Contents

Introduction

by Ken Ham

You probably know that word *chutzpah*. (A similar term is *audacity*.) I am using that Yiddish word to describe the actions of an atheist who visited our Creation Museum. He got in free by cheating, toured the museum, and afterward proceeded to blast the museum on his blog—a blog which is devoted to, as he calls it, "debunking Christianity."

How did he get in free? He played on the generosity and sympathy of a museum staff member. The man came to the museum desk and declared that he only had a short time to spend at the museum and did not have the money in his budget to pay for a ticket. Now, he did admit that he was skeptical of the museum's content. But the museum staff member, wanting to reach out to a person who expressed a financial need and also hoping the museum might challenge his thinking, allowed him in at no charge. We very much want skeptics to visit.

Conveniently, though, what didn't he tell her? Well, that he was really at the museum as an atheist who was wanting to go through the museum and then would be blasting it—without having to pay. We have since learned that the man has written five books in the past few years and advertises himself as a speaker against Christianity—I doubt very much he is the pauper he pretended to be when he came here.

But coming here under false pretenses and getting in free doesn't really upset me. Why? First, because he did hear God's Word throughout the museum, and "faith comes by hearing, and hearing by the word of God" (Romans 10:17). Perhaps this man will repent of his sins and believe in the Lord Jesus Christ.

Second, because he is an atheist, this man is only acting consistently with his worldview. I understand his actions, though I certainly don't condone them, for stealing is against all sorts of biblical teachings, including one of the Ten Commandments. But you see, he has no absolute standard by which he lives his life. So why is it even wrong in his secular worldview to misrepresent himself to us? He can justify being a cheater buy his atheistic religion.

So I understand his mindset. I really do. If there is no God, how could an atheist ever say what is right or wrong? By what standard can he make that determination? If each person decides for himself what is right or wrong, then he can argue that what he did at the museum was not wrong.

Secular atheistic humanism is a belief system about what we supposedly came from (nothing), what our purpose is in life (nothing), and what happens when we die (which again is nothing). Those who believe this way are only demonstrating the truth of Romans 1—they are suppressing the truth of God's existence in unrighteousness. They claim to be wise, but Romans 1 states that they have become fools.

It also did not make me mad when I learned that as this atheist was leaving the museum, he left a business card with our guest services staff member—the one who had been so kind to him. The card had the words "debunking Christianity" on it along with his website address. Now he wanted her to know what he was really doing at the museum, as if he was gloating, "Ha! I deceived you." But this behavior was consistent with his atheism.

I once posted a Facebook comment about this man, with the title, "Atheist debunking—or an advertisement for the Creation Museum?" Like most atheists who write negatively about their museum experience, he simply described some of the exhibits and, with lots of hand-waving, just said we were wrong. His lengthy piece really offered no real rebuttals of the scientific displays. He mocked the exhibits more than anything. (He did seem to be impressed with our Insectorium's collection of insects, though.) But I'm not upset with him for another reason: the man seems to have a lot of followers (based on the number of comments he is receiving about his blog against us), and so I see his blog post as an advertisement for the Creation Museum.

This atheist certainly saw and heard God's Word in the museum, and we should pray for him. I understand that he comes from a church background, but apparently he did not receive any effective apologetics teaching, or perhaps it may have been weak teaching. I don't know. So let's pray for this atheist, that God will use His Word to convict him and lead him to salvation through the Holy Spirit.

Meanwhile, because of cheaters like this man, we greatly tightened up our procedures to make sure that people like this don't take advantage of our generosity just so they can mock us. Actually, this museum incident shows he did not come to the Creation Museum with any other intent but to mock and speak against Christianity. Even before his visit, his atheistic, blind-faith religion had already biased what he would write about the Creation Museum!

We've had a number of instances of atheists not telling the truth (for them there is no such thing as "truth" anyway) in order to take advantage of us at the Creation Museum. For instance, TV commentator and comedian Bill Maher and his video crew lied and broke the rules to sneak into AiG.[1] And then there was an incident in 2010.[2] And there have been other instances. Actually, the atheists' behavior just illustrates Romans 1 over and over again—they work to suppress the truth because they know in their hearts that God created (Romans 1:18–19).

1. "HBO's Bill Maher and the plot to deceive AiG," February 7, 2007, blogs.answersingenesis. org/blogs/ken-ham/2007/02/07/hbos-bill-maher-and-the-plot-to-deceive-aig/.

2. "Attempted Crashing of 'Date Night' at the Creation Museum," February 15, 2011, www. answersingenesis.org/articles/2011/02/15/crashing-date-night.

Atheists Outline Their Global Religious Agenda

by Ken Ham

*I*n June 2010, atheists met at a conference in Copenhagen and released what they call their "Copenhagen Declaration on Religion in Public Life,"[1] which really means they released their statement of faith and their declaration against Christianity.

Their declaration is reprinted below (**in bold**), which is interspersed with my translation (regular font) on what they actually mean. These atheists think they can indoctrinate the public by their statements, but many are awake (and hopefully this short chapter will help even more people to awaken) to their agenda to indoctrinate the public in their anti-God religion.

Copenhagen Declaration on Religion in Public Life

We, at the World Atheist Conference: "Gods and Politics", held in Copenhagen from 18 to 20 June 2010, hereby declare [our Statement of Faith] **as follows:**

We recognize the unlimited right—even though we have no objective basis for "rights" in our system—**to freedom of conscience, religion, and belief**—except for Christians—**and that freedom to practice one's religion should be limited only by the need to respect the rights of others**—this is the golden rule: "do unto others . . . " for which we have no logical basis in our way of thinking; and except for Christians, as we reject Christianity totally and must try to eliminate it.

This is our dogma—**We submit that public policy should be informed by evidence**—except we discount the Bible as evidence—**and reason**—as long as it is autonomous human reason, as we arbitrarily reject the biblical God totally—**not by dogma**—except for our dogma of course, as we reject the claim of the absolute authority of the Christian God.

We assert the need for a society based on democracy—even though this has no logical basis in our evolutionary worldview where survival of the fittest dominates; and as long as the absolutes of Christianity are not allowed—**human rights**—for which we have no basis—**and the rule of law**—which protects the weak from the strong, despite the fact that we believe in evolution, which is about the strong dominating the weak. **History has shown that the most successful**—"successful" by our arbitrary dogma—**societies are the most secular**—just like the countries led by Mao, Pol Pot, Hitler, Mussolini, Lenin, and many more, killing off millions of human animals for their cause.

We assert—that is, we take the non-neutral position—**that the only equitable system**—even though we have no logical basis for what is fair—**of government in a democratic society is based on secularism**—the religion of naturalism and atheism, and thus relative morality, rejecting any absolutes (except we absolutely reject Christianity and the Bible)—**state neutrality in matters of religion or belief**—by which we mean the state must enforce our view, that is why we are absolutely against any absolute morality based on the Christian God—**favoring none**—except the religion of naturalism/atheism which is the only favored religious system—**and discriminating against none**—except Christians, as it is okay to discriminate against them because by our own arbitrary definitions we have eliminated Christianity, belief in a Creator God, and the claims of the Bible as God's revelation, thus it is okay to discriminate against Christians.

We assert that private conduct—except for Christians—**which respects the rights of others**—even though we have no basis for determining what "respect" means, nor any logical basis for why people (who are chance conglomerations of chemicals) ought to have "rights"—**should not be the subject of legal sanction or government concern**—unless it involves Christians, as we have determined they should not be allowed freedom for their religion because they believe in absolutes and have a system of absolute morality.

We affirm the right of believers and non-believers alike to participate in public life—as long as Christians do not use their position to act or even vote in accord with their Christian morality etc., as in public life they must act and vote in accord with what we call neutrality, which is really our religion of atheism and naturalism, because that is what we demand be imposed on our culture—**and their right to equality of treatment in the democratic process**—as long as they agree with our atheistic religion; otherwise, they are not allowed equality and must be marginalized and eliminated.

We affirm the right to freedom of expression for all—except for Christians, who cannot express their beliefs in public and certainly not in public schools, though it is okay for Muslims and atheists to indoctrinate kids in the public school system, but Christians can't even mention the Bible or their Christianity or they will be fired—**subject to limitations only as prescribed in international law**—which we will determine, as we reject the Bible—**laws which all governments should respect and enforce**—even though we have no basis for any laws except our opinion, if we can impose that. **We reject all blasphemy laws**—except for those which protect our religious belief in atheism and evolution, which must not be criticized as we have determined that it is okay to blaspheme the Christian God (though we try to avoid speaking against the Muslim god or others) because we have, by our arbitrary definitions, determined there is no God anyway—**and restrictions on the right to criticize religion or nonreligious life stances**—as long as no one criticizes atheism, because we have determined that this is fact and therefore any other position is outlawed if we can get away with that, as we are totally intolerant of others who don't have our position.

We assert the principle of one law for all—which is our law, which is arbitrary because we have no basis for it except that we want to impose it—**with no special treatment for minority communities**—except ours, even though we have no ultimate basis for such a belief—**and no jurisdiction for religious courts for the settlement of civil matters or family disputes**—which means no Christians can be involved in such courts because we reject Christianity; therefore, only courts based on our atheism and relative morality can inconsistently rule on such matters imposing their atheistic opinions on others.

We reject all discrimination in employment (other than for religious leaders)—as no one has a right to impose any morality on their organization except our system of morality (which is arbitrary, of course) and is against Christians. And of course we want to have atheists as leaders in atheist organizations so we need that freedom for our leaders—though in the organization itself we allow freedom, except for Bible-believing Christians of course as they have (by our arbitrary definition) been eliminated anyway—**and the provision of social services on the grounds of race, religion or belief, gender, class, caste or sexual orientation**—as we are tolerant of all; except we are intolerant of those dogmatic Christians who claim they have an absolute morality based on the Bible, which of course we reject as we want our own absolutes (which deny Christian absolutes) imposed on the culture.

We reject any special consideration for religion in politics and public life—except for the religion of atheism, as we want to control politics and public life and impose our arbitrary relative morality and intolerant system on the culture—**and oppose charitable, tax-free status and state grants for the promotion of any religion**—except the religion of atheism, as we want all the grants and the tax-free status—**as inimical to the interests of non-believers and those of other faiths. We oppose state funding for faith schools**—except for the atheist faith, as that is the only faith allowed in schools to be funded, which is why it is now really the official religion of the public schools in the USA, where Christianity by and large has been thrown out and replaced with the religion of naturalism/atheism, which is what we want to happen to all schools. That way, we can control the coming generations and indoctrinate them in atheism and against Christianity, which we are doing quite successfully at the present time.

We support the right to secular education—which means atheist-based education, as we totally reject Christian education because we are atheists out to impose our religion of atheism on the culture—**and assert the need for education in critical thinking**—except for naturalism/evolution; evolution is not allowed to be critically analyzed, because we need to indoctrinate kids totally in evolution so they will more easily accept our religion of atheism—**and the distinction between faith and reason as a guide to knowledge**—except for our faith in atheism, which we simply redefine as "reason," as we reject knowledge claimed to be from God and only allow knowledge to be determined based on our arbitrary definitions of science being naturalism—**and in the diversity of religious beliefs**—as long as Christianity is not allowed, because we are tolerant of all religions except Christianity. **We support the spirit of free inquiry**—except no one is free to base their beliefs on the Bible—**and the teaching of science free from religious interference**—except for the religion of atheism, as by our definition, science can only explain things based on natural causes, because we have by definition eliminated the supernatural from any part of science—**and are opposed to indoctrination, religious or otherwise**—except for the indoctrination in atheism/naturalism, which is what we are determined to do, and as long as we don't allow people to even consider the Bible or Christianity because atheism is the religion we demand be imposed on everyone, as we totally reject the God of the Bible.

---

1. See the text of the declaration at rationalwiki.org/wiki/Copenhagen_Declaration_on_Religion_in_Public_Life.

Ken Ham, President and CEO, Answers in Genesis & the Creation Museum

Ken earned a bachelor's degree in applied science from the Queensland Institute of Technology in Australia. He also holds a diploma of education from the University of Queensland. In recognition of his contribution to the church in the USA and internationally, Ken has been awarded two honorary doctorates: a Doctor of Divinity (1997) from Temple Baptist College in Cincinnati, Ohio and a Doctor of Literature (2004) from Liberty University in Lynchburg, Virginia.

Evolutionary Humanism: The Bloodiest Religion Ever

by Bodie Hodge

Man's authority or God's authority . . . two religions

If God and His Word are not the authority . . . then by default . . . who is? *Man* is. When people reject God and His Word as the ultimate authority, then man is attempting to elevate his or her thoughts (collectively or individually) to a position of authority *over* God and His Word.

So often, people claim that "Christians are religious and the enlightened unbelievers who reject God are *not* religious." Don't be deceived by such a statement. For these nonbelievers are indeed religious—*very* religious, whether they realize it or not. For they have bought into the religion of humanism.

Humanism is the religion that elevates man to be greater than God. Humanism, in a broad sense, encompasses any thought or worldview that rejects God and the 66 books of His Word in part or in whole; hence *all* non-biblical religions have humanistic roots. There are also those that *mix* aspects of humanism with the Bible. Many of these religions (e.g., Mormonism, Islam, Judaism, etc.) openly borrow from the Bible, but they also have mixed *human* elements into their religion where they take some of man's ideas to supersede many parts of the Bible, perhaps in subtle ways.[1]

There are many forms of humanism, but secular humanism has become one of the most popular today. Variant forms of secular humanism include atheism, agnosticism, non-theism, Darwinism, and the like. Each shares a belief in an evolutionary worldview with man as the centered authority over God.

Humanism organizations can also receive a tax-exempt status (the same as a Christian church in the United States and the United Kingdom) and they even have religious documents like the *Humanist Manifesto*. Surprisingly, this religion has free rein in state schools, museums, and media under the guise of neutrality, seeking to fool people into thinking it is not a "religion."[2]

Humanism and "good"

Christians are often confronted with the claim that a humanistic worldview will help society become "better."[3] Even the first *Humanist Manifesto*, of which belief in evolution is a subset, declared: "The goal of humanism is a free and universal society in which people voluntarily and intelligently co-operate for the common good."

But can such a statement be true? For starters, what do the authors mean by "good"? They have no legitimate foundation for such a concept, since one person's "good" can be another's "evil." To have some objective standard (not a relative standard), they must *borrow* from the absolute and true teachings of God in the Bible.

Beyond that, does evolutionary humanism really teach a future of prosperity and a common good? Since death is the "hero" in an evolutionary framework, then it makes one wonder. What has been the result of evolutionary thinking in the past century (20th Century)? Perhaps this could be a test of what is to come.

Let's first look at the death estimates due to aggressive conflicts stemming from leaders with evolutionary worldviews, beginning in the 1900s, to see the hints of what this "next level" looks like:

Table 1: Estimated deaths as a result of an evolutionary worldview

Who/What?	Specific event and estimated dead	Total Estimates
Pre-Hitler Germany/ Hitler and the Nazis	WWI: 8,500,000[4] WWII: 70 million[5] [Holocaust: 17,000,000][6]	95,000,000
Leon Trotsky and Vladimir Lenin	Bolshevik revolution and Russian Civil War: 15,000,000[7]	15,000,000
Joseph Stalin	20,000,000[8]	20,000,000
Mao Zedong	14,000,000 – 20,000,000[9]	Median estimate: 17,000,000
Korean War	2,500,000?[10]	~2,500,000
Vietnam War (1959-1975)	4,000,000 – 5,000,000 Vietnamese, 1,500,000 – 2,000,000 Lao and Cambodians[11]	Medians of each and excludes French, Australia, and U.S. losses: 6,250,000
Pol Pot (Saloth Sar)	750,000-1,700,000[12]	Median estimate: 1,225,000
Abortion to children[13]	China estimates since 1971-2006: 300,000,000[14] USSR estimates from 1954-1991: 280,000,000[15] US estimates 1928-2007: 26,000,000[16] France estimates 1936-2006: 5,749,731[17] United Kingdom estimates 1958-2006: 6,090,738[18] Germany estimates 1968-2007: 3,699,624[19]	621,500,000 and this excludes many other countries
Grand estimate		~778,000,000

Charles Darwin's view of molecules-to-man evolution was catapulted into societies around the world in the mid-to-late 1800s. Evolutionary teachings influenced Karl Marx, Leon Trotsky, Adolf Hitler, Pol Pot, Mao Zedong, Joseph Stalin, Vladimir Lenin, and many others. Let's take a closer look at some of these people and events and examine the evolutionary influence and repercussions.

World War I and II, Hitler, Nazis, and the Holocaust

Most historians would point to the assassination of Archduke Francis Ferdinand on June 18, 1914, as the event that triggered World War I (WWI). But tensions were already high considering the state of Europe at the time. Darwinian sentiment was brewing in Germany. Darwin once said:

> At some future period, not very distant as measured by centuries, the civilized races of man will almost certainly exterminate and replace the savage races throughout the world. At the same time the anthropomorphous apes . . . will no doubt be exterminated. The break between man and his nearest allies will then be wider, for it will intervene between man in a more civilized state, as we may hope, even than the Caucasian, and some ape as low as a baboon, instead of as now between the negro or Australian [Aborigine] and the gorilla.[20]

Darwin viewed the "Caucasian" (white-skinned Europeans) as the dominant "race" in his evolutionary worldview. To many evolutionists at the time, mankind had evolved from ape-like creatures that had more hair, dark skin, dark eyes, etc. Therefore, more "evolved" meant less body hair, blond hair, blue eyes, etc. Later, in Hitler's era, Nazi Germany practiced *Lebensborn*, which was a controversial program, the details of which have not been entirely brought to light. Many claim it was a breeding program that tried to evolve the "master race" further—more on this below.

But the German sentiment prior to WWI was very much bent on conquering for the purpose of expanding their territory and their "race." An encyclopedia entry from 1936 states:

> In discussions of the background of the war much has been said of Pan-Germanism, which was the spirit of national consciousness carried to the extreme limit. The Pan-Germans, who included not only militarists, but historians, scientists, educators and statesmen, conceived the German people, no matter where they located, as permanently retaining their nationality. The most ambitious of this group believed that it was their mission of Germans to extend their kultur (culture) over the world, and to accomplish this by conquest if necessary. In this connection the theory was advanced that the German was a superior being, destined to dominate other peoples, most of whom were thought of as decadent.[21]

Germany had been buying into Darwin's model of evolution and saw themselves as the superior "race," destined to dominate the world and their actions were the consequence of their worldview. This view set the stage for Hitler and the Nazi party and paved the road to WWII.

Hitler and the Nazis

World War II dwarfed World War I in the total number of people who died. Racist evolutionary attitudes exploded in Germany against people groups such as Jews, Poles, and many others. Darwin's teaching on evolution and humanism heavily influenced Adolf Hitler and the Nazis.

Hitler even tried to force the Protestant church in Germany to change fundamental tenants because of his newfound faith.[22] In 1936, while Hitler was in power, an encyclopedia entry on Hitler stated:

> . . . a Hitler attempt to modify the Protestant faith failed.[23]

His actions clearly show that he did not hold to the basic fundamentals taught in the 66 books of the Bible. Though some of his writings suggest he did believe in some form of God early on (due to his upbringing within Catholicism), his religious views moved toward atheistic humanism with his acceptance of evolution. Many atheists today try to disavow him but actions speak louder than words.

The Alpha History site (dedicated to much to the history of Nazi Germany by providing documents, transcribed speeches, and so on) says:

> Contrary to popular opinion, Hitler himself was not an atheist. . . . Hitler drifted away from the church after leaving home, and his religious views in adulthood are in dispute.[24]

So this history site is not sure what his beliefs were, but they seem to be certain that he was not an atheist! If they are not sure what beliefs he held, how can they be certain he was not an atheist?[25] The fact is that many people who walk away from church become atheists (i.e., they were never believers in the first place as 1 John 2:19 indicates). And Hitler's actions were diametrically opposed to Christianity . . . but not atheism, where there is no God who sets what is right and wrong.[26]

Regardless, this refutes notions that Hitler was a Christian as some have falsely claimed. Hitler's disbelief started early. He said:

> The present system of teaching in schools permits the following absurdity: at 10 a.m. the pupils attend a lesson in the catechism, at which the creation of the world is presented to them in accordance with the teachings of the Bible; and at 11 a.m. they attend a lesson in natural science, at which they are taught the theory of evolution. Yet the two doctrines are in complete contradiction. As a child, I suffered from this contradiction, and ran my head against a wall. . . . Is there a single religion that can exist without a dogma? No, for in that case it

would belong to the order of science. . . . But there have been human beings, in the baboon category, for at least three hundred thousand years. There is less distance between the man-ape and the ordinary modern man than there is between the ordinary modern man and a man like Schopenhauer . . . It is impossible to suppose nowadays that organic life exists only on our planet.[27]

Consider this quote in his unpublished second book:

The types of creatures on the earth are countless, and on an individual level their self-preservation instinct as well as the longing for procreation is always unlimited; however, the space in which this entire life process plays itself out is limited. It is the surface area of a precisely measured sphere on which billions and billions of individual beings struggle for life and succession. In the limitation of this living space lies the compulsion for the struggle for survival, and the struggle for survival, in turn contains the precondition for evolution.[28]

Hitler continues:

The history of the world in the ages when humans did not yet exist was initially a representation of geological occurrences. The clash of natural forces with each other, the formation of a habitable surface on this planet, the separation of water and land, the formation of the mountains, plains, and the seas. That [was] is the history of the world during this time. Later, with the emergence of organic life, human interest focuses on the appearance and disappearance of its thousandfold forms. Man himself finally becomes visible very late, and from that point on he begins to understand the term "world history" as referring to the history of his own development—in other words, the representation of his own evolution. This development is characterized by the never-ending battle of humans against animals and also against humans themselves.[29]

Hitler fully believed Darwin as well as Darwin's precursors—such as Charles Lyell's geological ages and millions of years of history. In his statements here, there is no reference to God. Instead, he unreservedly flew the banner of naturalism and evolution and only mentioned God in a rare instance to win Christians to his side, just as agnostic Charles Darwin did in his book *On the Origin of Species*.[30]

One part of the Nazi party political platform's 25 points in 1920 says:

> We demand freedom of religion for all religious denominations within the state so long as they do not endanger its existence or oppose the moral senses of the Germanic race. The Party as such advocates the standpoint of a positive Christianity without binding itself confessionally to any one denomination.[31]

Clearly this "positive Christianity" was an appeal to some of Christianity's morality, but not the faith itself. Many atheists today still appeal to a "positive Christian" approach, wanting the morality of Christianity (in many respects), but not Christianity.

Christianity was under heavy attack by Hitler and the Nazi's as documented from original sources prior to the end of WWII by Bruce Walker in *The Swastika against the Cross*.[32] The book clearly reveals the anti-Christian sentiment by Hitler and the Nazi's and their persecution of Christianity and their attempt to make Christianity change and be subject to the Nazi state and beliefs.

In 1939–1941, the Bible was rewritten for the German people at Hitler's command, eliminating all references to Jews and made Christ out to be pro-Aryan! The Ten Commandments were replaced with these twelve[33]:

1. Honor your Fuhrer and master.

2. Keep the blood pure and your honor holy.

3. Honor God and believe in him wholeheartedly.

4. Seek out the peace of God.

5. Avoid all hypocrisy.

6. Holy is your health and life.

7. Holy is your well-being and honor.

8. Holy is your truth and fidelity.

9. Honor your father and mother—your children are your aid and your example.

10. Maintain and multiply the heritage of your forefathers.

11. Be ready to help and forgive.

12. Joyously serve the people with work and sacrifice.

Hitler had *replaced* Christ in Nazi thought; and children were even taught to pray to Hitler instead of God![34] Hitler and the Nazi's were not Christian, but instead were humanistic in their outlook and any semblance of Christianity was cultic. The Nazi's determined that their philosophy was the best way to bring about the common good of all humanity.

Interestingly, it was Christians alone in Germany who were unconquered by the Nazi's and suffered heavily for it. Walker summarizes in his book:

> You would expect to find Christians and Nazis mortal enemies. This is, of course, exactly what happened historically. Christians, alone, proved unconquerable by the Nazis. It can be said that Christians did not succeed in stopping Hitler, but it cannot be said that they did not try, often at great loss and nearly always as true martyrs (people who could have chosen to live, but who chose to die for the sake of goodness.)[35]

Hitler and the Nazi's evolutionary views certainly helped lead Germany into WWII because they viewed the "Caucasian" as more evolved (and more specifically the Aryan peoples of the Caucasians), which to them justified their adoption of the idea that lesser "races" should be murdered in the struggle for survival. Among the first to be targeted were Jews, then Poles, Slavs, and then many others – including Christians regardless of their heritage.

Trotsky, Lenin

Trotsky and Lenin were both notorious leaders of the USSR—and specifically the Russian revolution. Lenin, taking power in 1917, became a ruthless leader and selected Trotsky as his heir. Lenin and Trotsky held to Marxism, which was built, in part, on Darwinism and evolution applied to a social scheme.

Karl Marx regarded Darwin's book as an "epoch-making book." With regard to Darwin's research on natural origins, Marx claimed, "The latter method is the only materialistic and, therefore, the only scientific one."[36]

Few realize or admit that Marxism, the primary idea underlying communism, is built on Darwinism and materialism (i.e., no God). In 1883, Freidrich Engels, Marx's longtime friend and collaborator, stated at Marx's funeral service that "Just as Darwin discovered the law of evolution in organic nature, so Marx discovered the law of evolution in human history."[37] Both Darwin and Marx built their ideologies on naturalism and materialism (tenants of evolutionary humanism). Trotsky once said of Darwin:

> Darwin stood for me like a mighty doorkeeper at the entrance to the temple of the universe. I was intoxicated with his minute, precise, conscientious and at the same time powerful, thought. I was the more astonished when I read . . . that he had preserved his belief in God. I absolutely declined to understand how a theory of the origin of species by way of natural selection and sexual selection and a belief in God could find room in one and the same head.[38]

Trotsky's high regard for evolution and Darwin were the foundation of his belief system. Like many, Trotsky probably did not realize that the precious few instances of the name "God" did not appear in the first edition of *Origin of Species*. These references were added later, and many suspect that this was done to influence church members to adopt Darwinism. Regardless, Trotsky may not have read much of Darwin's second book, *Descent of Man,* in which Darwin claims that man invented God:

> The same high mental faculties which first led man to believe in unseen spiritual agencies, then in fetishism, polytheism, and ultimately in monotheism, would infallibly lead him, as long as his reasoning powers remained poorly developed, to various strange superstitions and customs.[39]

Vladimir Lenin picked up on Darwinism and Marxism and ruled very harshly as an evolutionist. His variant of Marxism has become known as Leninism. Regardless, the evolutionist roots of Marx, Trotsky, and Lenin were the foundation that Communism has stood on—and continues to stand on.

Stalin, Mao, and Pol Pot, to name a few

Perhaps the most ruthless communist leaders were Joseph Stalin, Mao Zedong, and Pol Pot. Each of these were social Darwinists, ruling three different countries—the Soviet Union, China, and Cambodia respectively. Their reigns of terror demonstrated the end result of reducing the value of human life to that of mere animals, a Darwinistic teaching.[40] Though I could expand on each of these, you should be getting the point by now. So let's move to another key, but deadly, point in evolutionary thought.

Abortion—The war on babies

The war on children has been one of the quietest, and yet bloodiest, in the past hundred years. In an evolutionary mindset, the unborn have been treated as though they are going through an "animal phase" and can simply be discarded.

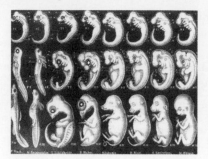 Early evolutionist Ernst Haeckel first popularized the concept that babies in the womb are actually undergoing animal developmental stages, such as a fish stage and so on. This idea has come to be known as *ontogeny recapitulates phylogeny*. Haeckel even faked drawings of various animals' embryos and had them drawn next to human embryos looking virtually identical.

These drawings have been shown to be completely false.[41] Haeckel himself partially confessed as much.[42] However, this discredited idea has been used repeatedly for a hundred years! Textbooks today still use this concept (though not Haeckel's drawings), and museums around the world still teach it.

Through this deception, many women have been convinced that the babies they are carrying in their wombs are simply going through an animal phase and can be aborted. Author Ken Ham, states:

> In fact, some abortion clinics in America have taken women aside to explain to them that what is being aborted is just an embryo in the fish stage of evolution, and that the embryo must not be thought of as human. These women are being fed outright lies.[43]

Evolutionary views have decreased the value of human life. Throughout the world the casualties of the war on children is staggering. Though deaths of children and the unborn did exist prior to the "evolution revolution," they have increased exponentially after the promotion of Darwinian teachings.

Conclusion

Is evolution the cause of wars and deaths? Absolutely not—both existed long before Darwin was born. Sin is the ultimate cause.[44] But an evolutionary worldview with its atheistic underpinnings has done nothing but add fuel to the fire.

In spite of the wars and atrocities caused by those who subscribed to an evolutionary worldview in recent times, there is still hope. We can end the seemingly endless atrocities against the unborn and those deemed less worthy of living, including the old and impaired.

In Egypt, Israelite boys were slaughtered by being thrown into the Nile at the command of Pharaoh (Exodus 1:20). And yet, by the providence of God, Moses survived and led the Israelites to safety, and the Lord later judged the Egyptians.

In Judea, under the Roman Empire, subordinate King Herod the Great commanded the slaughter of all the boys under the age of two in and around Bethlehem. And yet, by the providence of God, Jesus, the Son of God, survived and later laid down His life to bring salvation to mankind as the Prince of Peace. Herod's name, however, went down in history as an evil tyrant and murderer.

In this day and age, governments readily promote and fund the killing of children, both boys and girls, and sometimes command it, through abortion. By providence, however…you survived. While we can't change the past, we can learn from it. If we are to stop this continuing bloodshed, we must get back to the Bible and realize the bankrupt religion of evolutionary humanism has led only to death—by the millions. We need to point those who think humanity is the answer to the Savior who took the sins of humanity on Himself to offer them salvation.

---

1. For example: in Islam, Muhammad's words in the Koran are taken as a higher authority than God's Word (the Bible); in Mormonism, they have changed nearly 4,000 verses of the Bible to conform to Mormon teachings and add the words of Joseph Smith and later

prophets as superior to God's Word; in Judaism, they accept a portion of God's Word (the Old Testament) but by human standards, they reject a large portion of God's Word (the New Testament) as well as the ultimate Passover lamb, Jesus Christ.

2. Although the US Supreme Court says that religion is not to be taught in the classroom, this one seems to be allowed.

3. One can always ask the question, by what standard do they mean "better"? God is that standard so they refute themselves when they speak of things being better or worse. In their own professed worldview it is merely arbitrary for something to be "better" or "worse."

4. *The World Book Encyclopedia*, Volume 21, Entry: World War II, World Book, Inc., Chicago, IL, p. 467. Such statistics may have some variance depending on source as much of this is still in dispute.

5. Ranges from 60 to 80 million, so we are using 70 million.

6. Figures ranged from 7 to 26 million.

7. "Russian Civil War," en.wikipedia.org/wiki/Russian_Civil_War, October 23, 2008.

8. "Joseph Stalin," www.moreorless.au.com/killers/stalin.html, October 23, 2008.

9. "Mao Tse-Tung," www.moreorless.au.com/killers/mao.html, October 23, 2008.

10. This one is tough to pin down and several sources have different estimates, so this is a middle of the road estimate from the sources I found.

11. *The World Book Encyclopedia*, Volume 20, Entry: Vietnam War, World Book, Inc., Chicago, IL, p. 390.

12. "Pol Pot," en.wikipedia.org/wiki/Pol_Pot, October 23, 2008.

13. This table only lists estimates for abortion deaths in few countries; so, this total figure is likely very conservative.

14. "Historical abortion statistics, PR China," compiled by Wm. Robert Johnston, last updated 4 June 2008, www.johnstonsarchive.net/policy/abortion/ab-prchina.html.

15. "Historical abortion statistics, U.S.S.R.," compiled by Wm. Robert Johnston, last updated 4 June 2008, www.johnstonsarchive.net/policy/abortion/ab-ussr.html

16. "Historical abortion statistics, United States," compiled by Wm. Robert Johnston, last updated 4 June 2008, www.johnstonsarchive.net/policy/abortion/ab-unitedstates.html.

17. "Historical abortion statistics, France," compiled by Wm. Robert Johnston, last updated 4 June 2008, www.johnstonsarchive.net/policy/abortion/ab-france.html.

18. "Historical abortion statistics, United Kingdom," compiled by Wm. Robert Johnston, last updated 4 June 2008, www.johnstonsarchive.net/policy/abortion/ab-unitedkingdom.html.

19. "Historical abortion statistics, FR Germany," compiled by Wm. Robert Johnston, last updated 4 June 2008, www.johnstonsarchive.net/policy/abortion/ab-frgermany.html

20. Charles Darwin, *The Descent of Man*, New York: A.L. Burt, 1874, 2nd ed., p. 178.

21. *The American Educator Encyclopedia*, The United Educators, Inc., Chicago, 1936, p. 3914 under entry "World War."

22. *The American Educator Encyclopedia*, p. 1702 under entry "Hitler."

23. *The American Educator Encyclopedia*, p. 1494 under entry "Germany."

24. "Religion in Nazi Germany," alphahistory.com/nazigermany/religion-in-nazi-germany/, April 3, 2013.

25. Romans 1 makes it clear that all people believe in God, they just suppress that knowledge, and this is also the case with any professed atheist.

26. For an extensive treatise on Hitler's (and the Nazi's) religious viewpoints, see: J. Bergman, *Hitler and the Nazi Darwinian Worldview*, Joshua Press Inc., Kitchener, Ontario,

Canada, 2012.

27. "Hitler, Adolf, 1941," translated by Cameron, Norman and Stevens, R.H. *Hitler's Secret Conversations, 1941–1944*. The New American Library of World Literature, Inc., 1961.

28. *Hitler's Second Book*, Adolf Hitler, Edited by Gerald L. Weinberg, 2003 Enigma books, Translated by Krista Smith, p. 8.

29. *Hitler's Second Book*, p. 9.

30. In the first edition of *Origin of Species*, God is not mentioned, in the sixth edition "God" was added several times to draw Christians into this false religion. See R. Hedtke, *Secrets of the Sixth Edition*, Master Books, Green Forest, AR, 2010.

31. "Nazi Party 25 Points (1920)," alphahistory.com/nazigermany/nazi-party-25-points-1920/

32. B. Walker, *The Swastika against the Cross*, Outskirts Press, Inc., Denver, CO, 2008.

33. "Hitler rewrote the Bible and added two commandments," *Pravda* News Site, 8/10/2006, english.pravda.ru/world/europe/10-08-2006/83892-hitler-0/; "Jewish References erased in newly found Nazi Bible," *Daily Mail Online*, August 7, 2006, www.dailymail.co.uk/news/article-399470/Jewish-references-erased-newly-Nazi-Bible.html.

34. Walker, pp. 20–22.

35. Walker, p. 88.

36. *Great Books of the Western World*, Volume 50, Capital, Karl Marx, William Benton (Publishers), Chicago, 1952, Footnotes on p. 166 and p. 181.

37. G. Himmelfarb, *Darwin and the Darwinian Revolution*, London: Chatto & Windus, 1959, p. 348.

38. Max Eastman, *Trotsky: A portrait of his youth*, New York, pp. 117–118, 1925.

39. Charles Darwin, *The Descent of Man and Selection in Relation to Sex*, Chapter III (Mental Powers of Man and the Lower Animals), 1871, As printed in *Great Books of the Western World*, Volume 49, Robert Hutchins, Ed., Chicago, 1952, p. 303.

40. R. Hall, "Darwin's Impact—The Bloodstained Legacy of Evolution," *Creation* Magazine 27(2):46–47, March, 2005, www.answersingenesis.org/articles/cm/v27/n2/darwin.

41. Michael Richardson et al, *Anatomy and Embryology*, 196(2):91–106, 1997.

42. Haeckel said, "A small portion of my embryo-pictures (possibly 6 or 8 in a hundred) are really (in Dr. Brass's [one of his critics] sense of the word) "falsified"—all those, namely, in which the disclosed material for inspection is so incomplete or insufficient that one is compelled in a restoration of a connected development series to fill up the gaps through hypotheses, and to reconstruct the missing members through comparative syntheses. What difficulties this task encounters, and how easily the draughts—man may blunder in it, the embryologist alone can judge." "The Truth about Haeckel's Confession," *The Bible Investigator and Inquirer*, M.L. Hutchinson, Melbourne, March 11, 1911, p. 22–24.

43. Ken Ham, *The Lie: Evolution*, Chapter 8: The evils of evolution, Master Books, Green Forest, AK, 1987, p. 105.

44. *The New Answers Book 1*, Gen. Ed. Ken Ham, Master Books, Green Forest, Arkansas, 2006, Chapter 26: Why does God's creation include death and suffering?, pp. 325–338. www.answersingenesis.org/articles/nab/why-does-god's-creation-include-suffering.

What Are the Tactics of the New Atheists?

by Elizabeth Mitchell (with endnotes by Bodie Hodge)

Following the April 29, 2013 opening of their documentary *The Unbelievers* at Toronto's Hot Dog Film Festival, outspoken atheists Richard Dawkins and Lawrence Krauss discussed the merits of their approaches to "ridding the world of religion." In a recent interview with Steve Paikin, they made it clear that, despite their sometimes different personas, they have the same agenda—getting people to get rid of their belief in God.[1] Yet they both say that Christians should not feel "threatened" by their efforts to expunge religion from human history.

Outspoken atheists Lawrence Krauss and Richard Dawkins, co-stars of the documentary *The Unbelievers*, discuss their strategy for ridding the world of religion in general and Christianity in particular. They consider Christianity "demeaning" and wish to re-design society "the way we want it." Image: screen shots from interview with Steve Paikin on ww3.tvo.org/video/190768/rise-new-atheists.

The goal of *The Unbelievers* documentary

Evolutionary biologist Dawkins and theoretical physicist Krauss recounted that when they first met they had a heated debate about, as Dawkins said, "whether we should have a kind of full-on attack on religion or whether we should, as Lawrence preferred, seduce them."[2] Krauss explained that this is really "a strategic question."[3] They agree that both approaches have merit depending on the nature of the people being targeted. However, expressing general agreement with the more confrontational approach of the often-irascible Dawkins, Krauss said, "You've got to confront silly beliefs by telling them they are silly," adding, "If you're trying to convince people, pointing out that what they believe is nonsense is a better way to bring them around."[4]

Despite their great hostility toward religious beliefs (other than their own) and avowal that they hope this film will help in their efforts to eradicate all religion worldwide, the atheist pair indicates that belief or non-belief in a deity is not what really matters to them. Krauss declares that what is actually important to them is that "everything should be open to question and that the universe is a remarkable place."[5] By contrast, he says, "This is more important to us than not believing in God—that's not important at all."

Dawkins and Krauss both expressed grudging tolerance for evolutionists who want to keep their religious beliefs in order to keep the good things religion offers them—"spirituality," "consolation," and "community"—so long as they do not then reject evolution.[6] They said that people are "hard-wired" to seek something spiritual, but by "spiritual" they refer to a sort of emotional high. And they declare that science offers a better kind of spirituality, "a sense of oneness with the universe."[7] Therefore science[8], they maintain, can meet the inmost needs of people better than religion of any sort.

"Spirituality is a sense of awe and wonder at something bigger than oneself,"[9] Krauss explained, adding that being "insignificant is uplifting."[10] And while some people cling to their religion to satisfy some spiritual need,[11] he says, "The spirituality of science is better than the spirituality of religion because it is real."[12] Both of course vigorously deny that their own atheistic position is one of "belief," saying "we don't define ourselves by what we don't believe in."

Dawkins and Krauss want to rid the world of all religion except their own

Like most atheists, Dawkins and Krauss fail to recognize the worldview-based nature of the interpretations they define as "real." They repeatedly refer in the interview to accepting the "evidence of reality" concerning origins when they are actually equating their worldview-based interpretations with reality. Furthermore, the atheistic belief that there is no God is actually a "religion."

There really is no such thing as a person without a religion—you either believe that there is or is not a god. You are either for Christ or against Him (Luke 11:23), and you base your interpretation of origins, morality, and the meaning of life on that belief. The belief that there is or is not a god is essential to how one explains existence, the nature of authority, and our place in the universe. Krauss's belief that the atoms in his body originated billions of years ago in stardust, for instance, is the "religious" way he explains his existence without God and the way he experiences what passes for spirituality by knowing the "fantastic" truth that he is "intimately connected to the cosmos."

Atheists do claim to be non-religious, but they use their set of beliefs as a way to explain life without God—they worship and serve the creation (e.g., the universe) rather than the Creator (Romans 1:25). Krauss extols the profound sense of wonder he gets studying the cosmos and Dawkins enjoys the "poetry of science," but they tie their love for science to their belief in atheistic evolution and their sheer joy in shaking their fists at the possibility of a Creator's existence.

The reason behind the hostility toward religion

And frankly, the point here is not whether a person defines their worldview as a religion or not, or whether he believes in a "god." Christianity is unique—it is the truth—and, perhaps for that reason as much as any other, is the especial target for Dawkins and most others. Those who love "darkness" (e.g., sin, rebellion against God, and rejection of Jesus Christ) will naturally attack the light (John 3:19–21). Based on Scripture, we know that God looks at the heart to see how each person stands in relation to Jesus Christ (Romans 10:9–10; cf. 1 Samuel 16:7). Again, Jesus made clear that a person is either for or against Him (Matthew 12:30; 25:46).

Dawkins and Krauss reserve their greatest hostility for young-earth creationists. They indicated that all debate about origins has been completely settled by "Darwin and his successors"[13] and by big bang cosmology,[14] which Krauss describes as "the last bastion of God—I mean there are some fundamentalists of course who say the earth is 6,000 years old and don't believe in evolution—but rational 'theologians' have moved away from that debate."[15]

Design in nature

Furthermore, even Dawkins admits that nature—in particular, biology—appears to be specially designed. We see, for instance, precise irreducible complexity everywhere we look, from major anatomical features to biological processes at the molecular level. Dawkins agrees that "special creation" is "intuitive"—a look at nature in essence screams that there must have been a Creator.

But Dawkins says that he is thankful to Darwin for coming up with a very "*non-intuitive*" way to explain nature without God. Darwinian belief basically builds a theoretical guess about biological origins by appealing to a series of billions of tiny, unobservable changes over billions of unobserved years.[16] Yet neither Darwin nor his successors have through scientific observation shown how either abiogenesis or the evolution of biological complexity is possible.

Dawkins explains that both biology and physics (cosmology) are complementary fields that supplant belief in God.[17] But he indicated that biology, because design is so apparent, was the first battleground in the war against a Creator. He said the following:

> Historically biology, I suppose, has been the most fertile ground for those who wish to make a supernatural account because living things are so fantastically complicated and beautiful and elegant, and they carry such an enormous weight of apparent design. They really look as though they're designed.
>
> So historically biology has been the most fertile ground for theological arguments. That's all solved now. Darwin and his successors solved that.
>
> I think the spotlight in a way has shifted to physics and to cosmology where we're less confident I think about how the universe began—in one way more confident because there's a lot of detailed mathematical modeling going one—but there are some profound questions remaining to be answered in that field and that's where cosmologists like Lawrence come in. We are complementary.

In typical fashion, Krauss and Dawkins believe that anyone who disagrees with their own interpretations about origins is irrational and out of touch with reality. And as happens with most lay people, anything that can be "mathematically modeled" is accepted as truth because numbers surely do not lie. Yet mathematical models concerning cosmology (like the big bang) and the long-age interpretations ascribed to radiometric dating are based on unverifiable, worldview-based assumptions.[18]

Dawkins and Krauss say that they hope that viewers of their film will be inspired by the wonders of science to critically evaluate their beliefs and to acknowledge that they are "silly." As discussed below however, from a biblical worldview, a careful study of the wonders of science only affirms what God reveals in the Bible and actually glorifies the Creator (Psalm 19:1; Colossians 1:16–17).

Biblical creationists understand that God created all the various kinds of living organisms about 6,000 years ago (based on the genealogies listed in the Bible). According to Genesis chapter one, God equipped each to reproduce "after their kinds." There is no indication in Scripture that God used evolutionary processes or that He made organisms able to evolve through random processes into new and increasingly complex kinds of creatures. We also do not see this happen in biology.

Organisms vary within their kinds (e.g., variations in dogs or in cats) but do not evolve into new, more complex kinds of organisms (e.g., amoebas into dogs or cats). Bacteria remain bacteria, canines remain canines, apes remain apes, and humans remain humans—though there is much biodiversity among each created kind. This diversification within kinds is observable. But evolution of new kinds is not, and biological observation can offer no actual mechanisms by which this can happen.[19]

Further, biological observation confirms that living things do not spring into existence through the random interaction of non-living components, despite evolutionary claims about abiogenesis. This is consistent with the biblical account of our origins. Thus, biblical history—God's eyewitness account of what He did when He created us and what sort of biology He put in motion—does not differ from biological observations. There is nothing "irrational" about recognizing that observable science is consistent with biblical history.[20]

Can Dawkins and Krauss really "rid this world of religion"?

The interviewer concluded by asking the pair, "Is it your hope or expectation that you can, in your words, rid this world of religion?"

"I'm not sure how soon," Dawkins answered. "I think that religion is declining, that Christianity is declining throughout Christendom."[21] Looking to the future, he adds, "And I think that that's going to continue. If we look at the broad sweep of history, it's clear that the trend is going in the right direction. I'm not so optimistic that it will be in my lifetime, but it will happen."[22]

And what do Dawkins and Krauss hope to accomplish by getting rid of Christianity? Why do they care what others believe? Why are they so eager to expedite God's exit from human history? Dawkins summed up the proud position of humanism when he said that he wants to see us "intelligently design our society, our ethics, our morality—so that we live in the kind of society we want to live in rather than in the kind of society that was laid down in a book written in 800 BC."[23] Krauss added that accepting the ideas of "Iron Age peasants" is "demeaning."[24]

Though Dawkins and Krauss disparage the ideas of biblical peasants, their notions of social planning really sound very much like the post-Flood population who built the Tower of Babel in rebellion against God's command to replenish the earth. In their pride (Psalm 10:4; Proverbs 16:8), those people said, "Let us make a name for ourselves" (Genesis 11:4). Indeed, how arrogant does a person have to be to assume that everyone who disagrees with him is either ill-informed or irrational? Is it any wonder that God hates pride, for through humanistic pride people not only reject God's ways but "suppress the truth" (Romans 1:18) of His very existence?

Dawkins and Krauss seem to want to redesign the world and society for the rest of us according to their own vision, making certain that God is written out of the picture. Yet those of us who know and trust God and accept the Bible as His revealed Word believe wholeheartedly that Jesus Christ, our Creator and Savior, possesses all true wisdom and knowledge (Colossians 1:16–17, 3:2). And we not only accept the history in God's Word but also God's declaration that we are all sinners in need of the grace of Jesus Christ. By contrast, those who, like Dawkins and Krauss, refuse to even acknowledge the testimony of the "design" they themselves see in nature (Romans 1:18–22) and their own consciences (Romans 2:12–16), much less God's Word, are—according to God—"fools" (Psalm 14:1, 53:1). "Professing to be wise, they became fools" (Romans 1:22).

In answer to the interviewer's final question about the prospects for the imminent demise of religion, Krauss said, "I would have thought that by now religion would be gone. I thought religion was on the way out [in the 1960s], so I was kind of surprised and disappointed in some ways by the resurgence of fundamentalism in my country [the United States]."[25] Speaking of the future he expects, he adds, "But I do think that it's obvious that access to information and knowledge is decreasing" the number of people who say they are religious worldwide and that "inevitably knowledge and wonder of the real universe will supplant" religion.[26] Answers in Genesis exists to make knowledge available to help people make informed decisions about the claims of atheistic evolutionists so that they will see that they can trust God's Word from the very first verse.

Both Krauss and Dawkins think it unreasonable that people feel "threatened" by their efforts to rid the world of religion.[27] Dawkins said, "where religion is concerned if you speak clearly it sounds threatening" and "if you say something clearly and distinctly and truthfully there are people who will take that as threatening." He said that religion is so entrenched that it "gets a free ride" and that "very mild criticism" and "questioning" shouldn't be regarded as threatening.[28]

Conclusion: man's word vs. God's Word

Krauss and Dawkins repeatedly refer to the "evidence of reality" in this interview. Yet they, like other evolutionary scientists, fail to distinguish between testable scientific reality—experimental science—and the untestable, unobservable, and unverifiable assumptions on which the scientific claims of evolutionary origins science are based. What they claim as "reality" is interpreted through their own worldview, a worldview that is clearly hostile toward God.[29]

And while they oppose "all" religion, it is clear they particularly oppose Christianity and the Bible. They firmly believe that anyone who fails to accept their worldview is irrational. They admit that religion meets the needs of some people for "spirituality," but their concept of spirituality is a purely emotional response.[30]

And lest this "response" be deemed defensive (a point made not only in this interview but also by a number of atheists who have recently written in to this ministry), let me hasten to point out that if "just asking a question" should not be seen as "threatening," then neither should just answering one. If saying "something clearly and distinctly and truthfully" should not be seen as threatening when Dawkins speaks, then neither should the truth from God's Word be taken that way. It should not be threatening when we question evolution, big bang, millions of years, humanism, or even Dawkins and Krauss themselves. In fact, they would welcome it in every forum, if they were consistent.

Krauss and Dawkins do have one thing in common with most biblical creationists—a sense of awe and wonder at what we can learn from experimental science about the world around us. Krauss and Dawkins appreciate the "poetry of science" but superimpose their own rhapsodic notions about the atoms in our bodies being derived from stardust billions of years old.[31] Biblical creationists, however, examine the actual facts of science—the observable and repeatable ones, not evolutionary story telling and conjectures—in light of God's revealed truth and see that there actually is no contradiction between the history revealed in the Bible and science (Romans 1:18–22).

Krauss and Dawkins hope their film will prompt Christians to ask questions and to critically examine their beliefs in light of science. At Answers in Genesis we encourage people—both believers and unbelievers—to ask questions and to critically examine Scriptural revelation and scientific facts. We provide help in finding answers to those questions.

Sadly, one example Dawkins provided was a young-earth creationist who came to his lectures on evolution and was very impressed, having never heard the evolutionary point of view. We do not encourage ignorance about evolutionary positions[32] but instead want to equip people with the information they need to discern the difference between observable experimental science and historical science, between that which can be tested and that which can only be imagined, between what can actually be seen in the world through science and the claims of evolutionists.

We want to equip children, teens, and adults with the tools they need to help them trust God's Word and see through false religions like atheism, so that they will then be able to trust Jesus Christ as their Savior and the Lord of their lives. The very name of our ministry, Answers in Genesis, makes it clear we are not encouraging people to have blind faith. On the contrary, we are providing reasonable, scientific, and biblical answers for questions on origins. And we do so with confidence that the Bible has the answers to explain the world we live in—scientifically, morally, and theologically.

The Bible attests not only to the true history of our origins but also the truth about humanity's rebellious and sinful nature.[33] Dawkins and Krauss consider biblical truth restrictive and demeaning. The Bible does make it clear that all people are sinners who have rebelled against the omniscient, omnipotent, and holy God.

Dawkins and Krauss personify this rebellious spirit in declaring their desire to redesign the world the way "we"—in other words, "they"—want it to be. But evil men and seducers will, according to Scripture, get worse and worse (2 Timothy 3:13), so much so that Jesus said "Nevertheless, when the Son of Man comes, will He really find faith on the earth?" (Luke 18:8).

As Christians, meanwhile, we are commanded to respond to the "nonthreatening threats" volleyed at us by skeptics and by sincere questioners by providing answers (1 Peter 3:15, KJV; 2 Timothy 2:22–26), including the answer to people's sin problem (Romans 3:23, 6:23)—salvation through the shed blood of Jesus Christ. But the final end of humanity's destiny is not the end prophesied by Dawkins and Krauss, for the same Jesus Christ that rose from the dead will indeed come again (Revelation 22:20). Dawkins and Krauss may be leading the charge to eradicate Christianity, but it is the Lord Jesus Christ who will surely have the last word.

---

1. ww3.tvo.org/video/190768/rise-new-atheists.

2. Of course, Dawkins means all religions but his own. He is very religious being a secular humanist. He is a signer of the Humanist Manifesto III. Humanism comes in various flavors like "agnosticism," "traditional atheism," "new atheism," and so on. When someone says he is "not religious" in this context, that is a fancy way of saying he adheres to the religion of humanism in one form or another. Dawkins's religious viewpoint is "new atheism." It is distinguished from traditional atheism in that it actively proselytizes for the atheistic point of view, whereas adherents of traditional atheism believe that nothing matters and so see no reason to proselytize.

3. We have known about their strategic attacks for some time. They have tried to force the religion of humanism in the classroom and now elsewhere. In 1983, humanist John Dunphy spoke of this strategy—to put their atheistic religion into schools—when he said: "I am convinced that the battle for humankind's future must be waged and won in the public school classroom by teachers who correctly perceive their role as the proselytizers of a new faith: a religion of humanity that recognizes and respects the spark of what theologians call divinity in every human being. These teachers must embody the same selfless dedication as the most rabid fundamentalist preachers, for they will be ministers of another sort, utilizing a classroom instead of a pulpit to convey humanist values in whatever subject they teach, regardless of the educational level—preschool, daycare, or large state university. The classroom must and will become an arena of conflict between the old and the new-the rotting corpse of Christianity, together with all its adjacent evils and misery, and the new faith of humanism." John Dunphy, "A Religion for a New Age," quoted in John Dunphy, "The Book that Started It All," Council for Secular Humanism, www.secularhumanism.org/index.php?section=library&page=dunphy_21_4.

4. Yet these atheists do not realize the silliness of their own views. Dawkins himself admits that it is possible that aliens designed and seeded life on earth—yes, really!

Krauss and Dawkins both believe that all people ultimately came from a rock—clearly this is in violation of the Law of Biogenesis. Both believe that everything is material; therefore, from their view, logic, truth, and knowledge, which are non-material, cannot exist. By thus laying claim to logic, truth, and knowledge, they inadvertently borrow from a Christian worldview—how silly for their religion to borrow from its enemy! Dawkins argues there is no morality and then tries to say Christians are immoral. Both believe that nothing ultimately matters; yet they both seem to think it matters a great deal to force this belief on others. Neither Krauss nor Dawkins seem to realize that in an atheistic worldview, the atheist is actually claiming to be "God" (because to know there is no God, one must be omnipresent and omniscient, which are attributes of God alone), which refutes their own atheism. This short list should suffice. Such silliness should be embarrassing to an atheist.

5. Interestingly, Christians believe in asking questions and seeking answers to all sorts of tough questions—including the scientific and the theological. And Christians certainly recognize that the universe is a remarkable place, but we know it was created by God. So the opposition to Christianity on this ground is completely without warrant by their own criteria.

6. Evolution (and millions of years, or geological evolution) is the real key. These are tenets of the Humanist Manifestos, so humanists do not want to give up this key aspect. They must fight for this in their religion. But underlying all of this is the idea that man is the ultimate authority, not God.

7. "Oneness with the universe" is a tenet of Buddhism, which is strange considering they are arguing to oppose Buddhism along with all other religions.

8. What they mean by "science" here is not the observable and repeatable science that makes discoveries about how things work and applies that knowledge, but instead a "science" that embraces naturalism and evolution as absolutely axiomatic. Therefore, what Dawkins and Krauss mean when they say science is not just how things work but their own naturalistic, unverifiable, dogmatically-held ideas about where everything came from. By science, they really mean their religion of humanism.

9. If one believes there is something greater than oneself in atheism, then it means that he is not atheistic. Hence, this is self-refuting.

10. If being insignificant is so great, then why waste time seeking popularity by speaking out against Christianity by making documentaries?

11. This is oddly similar to what the religious atheist is doing, per the very context.

12. This is a "No True Scotsman" fallacy, meaning that the arguer has defined the terms in a biased way to protect his argument from rebuttals.

13. It is sad that they appeal to Darwin, a racist, who went so far as to say that the more evolved Caucasians would eventually exterminate everyone else (Charles Darwin, The Descent of Man [New York: A.L. Burt, 1874, 2nd ed.], p. 178). Even James Watson, a co-discoverer of the structure of DNA, also has underlying racist attitudes. But note that they appeal to man as the ultimate authority.

14. Which big bang model (open models, closed model) do they think is true and why are the others wrong?

15. The atheists simply do not like the fact that Christians actually believe God when He speaks. They really want us to compromise God's Word with theirs like Eve did in the garden and to deny God's Word in Genesis in favor of their fallible sinful words. The issue is not mere distaste for creationists, but rather their distaste for God's Word. Note this: the conflict is not between atheists and creationists; it is between atheists and God.

16. Note what replaced God in their religion. It was time, chance, and death. Without these, evolution is meaningless. These are the "god" for an evolutionary worldview.

17. Yet science comes out of a Christian worldview, where God upholds the universe in a particular fashion, and this all-knowing God has told us so (e.g., Genesis 8:22 and others). In the humanistic view, how can man know that the laws in the universe will be the same in the future? According to man, from the big bang to today, the laws have changed. How

does one know they will not change tomorrow? If one says, "because they always have," he is arbitrarily begging the question.

18. Such methods are classic cases of begging the question; they are using long-age assumptions to prove long ages. We could just as easily do the same thing by using young-age assumptions to prove a young earth, but this simply shows the arbitrariness of their uniformitarian claims.

19. The two proposed mechanisms of evolution are called: (1) natural selection, a creationist concept by the way, and (2) mutations. In both cases, they are losing information (i.e., it is going in the wrong direction for evolution). For example, natural selection filters out already existing information; mutations lose information quickly, or in many cases it remains nearly neutral. See www.answersingenesis.org/articles/nab/is-natural-selection-evolution and www.answersingenesis.org/articles/nab2/mutations-engine-of-evolution.

20. Isn't it fascinating that humanists who are materialistic by their very admission appeal to logic and claim we are irrational, when rational thought is only possible if nonmaterial things exist like concepts, truth, logic, and so on? Yet these atheists (materialists, humanists) must reject it because if they leave open an immaterial realm (i.e., a spiritual realm), then God could exist and they cannot be atheistic or humanistic (i.e., humans are the ultimate authority).

21. Yet Christianity is still the fastest growing religion. Please see fastestgrowingreligion.com/numbers.html; it is merely declining or stagnant in certain places, like Western Europe and the U.S.

22. Did you catch that Dawkins just made a prophecy? He predicted that religion would cease. God disagrees with Him (Matthew 16:18; Daniel 2:44).

23. Satan, in the Bible, sinned with his pride of wanting to ascend to God's position (Isaiah 14:14). It appears clear that Dawkins wants to replace God, too, as the "intelligent designer" no less, albeit of society rather than the universe. (We suppose even Dawkins knows he has some limitations!) Interestingly, Dawkins does seem to believe in a form of intelligent design because he has said he considers it a possibility that aliens designed life here (per his comments in the documentary *Expelled* with Ben Stein, not in this interview). Furthermore, it is unclear what book Dawkins is talking about, though he is surely alluding to the Bible with a prejudicial conjecture about the timing. The Bible was written over the course of about 1450 BC to about AD 68–95 (Christians do debate this). Take note of the irony here though; Dawkins wants people to follow what he says in his books, but not follow God's book! Again, he is trying to replace God (2 Corinthians 2:11), and in his own mind, he already has.

24. Note the straw man fallacies these atheists are committing. They are trying to make Christianity look silly, but because they cannot even get basic facts correct, they look silly by default.

25. This is reminiscent of atheist Friedrich Nietzsche who declared "God is dead" several times in the 1800s. It is sad that atheists like Krauss know so little about God's Word that they fail to realize a dominating principle: the power of God in the Resurrection. When the Jews had Christ crucified, even Christ's disciples thought the Son of God was dead. But God is known for His Resurrection. Though Nietzsche is dead, God continues to live and gives to all life and breath. And Christianity continues to grow by the power of the Holy Spirit.

26. Note here that Krauss has now prophesied the same sort of thing as Dawkins. He is predicting that universe worship, like his atheistic view, will come to destroy religion. But this would naturally fail, as atheism and universe worship are a form of religion, making Krauss's prediction inherently contradictory.

27. Actually, Christians should find it a blessing. Matthew 5:11 says, "Blessed are you when they revile and persecute you, and say all kinds of evil against you falsely for My sake."

28. Again, Christians do not fear questioning, nor do we get a free ride or mild criticism. Christians in various parts of the world are murdered for their beliefs, attacked and beaten for their beliefs, abused for their beliefs, and lied about because of their beliefs. If one is not a Christian, like Dawkins, why assume such people actually adhere to the Ten Commandments, which say not to lie? Dawkins claimed that there is no morality in his debate with

Lanier. So why trust him to tell the truth? With this in mind, notice Dawkins's deception here. He wants the freedom to question, but he does not want us to respond. Nor does he want Christians to question things like evolution or the big bang—especially in classrooms! If he did welcome responses, he would be happy for Christians to question evolution, the big bang, naturalism, and so on, and to respond to his false claims about Christianity in a proper forum, like the classroom, which is a place for learning. But Dawkins is adamant that Christians should have no say, no response, and no questioning of the evolutionary view in the state schools. Dawkins wants only his religion taught in schools and only his religion is permitted to question others. This is a double standard.

29. Remember, they assume long ages to prove long ages—an arbitrary begging the question fallacy.

30. They are trying to demote all religions to being materialistic (underlings to their religion). This is why they say spiritual is not immaterial, but merely emotion (e.g., chemical reaction in the brain). They are trying to change the definition of spirit and spiritual. They want to make God (who is spirit, John 4:24) into part of the universe or place Him in a position that is lower than the universe. Hence, the universe can be the unofficial "god" to the atheist, next to man, of course.

31. When Krauss attacks the Bible with his famous mantra, "Forget Jesus, the stars died so you can be here today," he is promoting a mere fairy tale and stories to satisfy a meaning-less atheistic worldview.

32. This is why we teach people about each evolutionary view and its problems. In brief, there are five main views: (1) The Epicurean evolutionary view, which has its roots in Greek mythology. This is where evolution came from. The newer forms we have today are just rehashes of this mythology that Paul refuted in Acts 17; (2) Lamarckian evolution, which taught that animals can acquire new traits through interactions with their environments, and then pass them on to the next generation; (3) Traditional Darwinism, where natural selection and time are the primary factors for change; (4) Neo-Darwinism, where natural selection and time are combined with mutations as the primary factors for evolution; and (5) Punctuated Equilibrium, which tries to explain the lack of fossil evidence for transitional forms. This view assumes that evolution occurred in bursts and is not recorded in the fossil layers; it still relies on natural selection, mutations, and time. For more, see Roger Patterson and Dr. Terry Mortenson, "Do Evolutionists Believe Darwin's Ideas about Evolution?" *New Answers Book 3*, Ken Ham, gen. ed. (Green Forest, AR: 2010), pp. 271–282.

33. It is important to note that in the beginning, God called His creation "very good" (Genesis 1:31; Deuteronomy 32:4). It is because of man's sin that death, suffering, and disease came into the creation. God did not make the world like it is today (full of suffering) but subjected it to this due to man's sin. We have essentially been given a taste of what life is like without God. But Christ did not leave us to perish; instead, he took the punishment that we deserve, once for all. Christ, the God-man, took the infinite punishment that is demanded by the very nature of God, who is infinite. God then offers the free gift of salvation, and promises a new heavens and new Earth that will not be subjected to death, suffering, and decay. See www.answersingenesis.org/articles/2009/04/21/what-does-it-mean-to-be-saved.

Elizabeth Mitchell, researcher and writer, Answers in Genesis

Dr. Mitchell received a bachelor of science in chemistry from Furman University in 1980. She graduated from Vanderbilt University School of Medicine in Nashville and completed her residency in obstetrics and gynecology at Vanderbilt University Affiliated Hospitals in 1988. Dr. Mitchell practiced medicine in Gallatin, Tennessee, but in 1995 she retired from private practice to devote herself more fully to the needs of her family.

Atheism: An Irrational Worldview

by Jason Lisle

Atheists are "coming out of the closet" and becoming more vocal about their message that "there is no God." Professor Richard Dawkins (Britain's leading atheist) is encouraging those who share his views to express their opinion. Author of *The God Delusion*, Dawkins says he wants to "free children from being indoctrinated with the religion of their parents or their community."[1] Will Christians be prepared to "give an answer" to the atheists' claims?[2]

Materialistic atheism is one of the easiest worldviews to refute. A materialistic atheist believes that nature is all that there is. He believes that there is no transcendent God who oversees and maintains creation. Many atheists believe that their worldview is rational—and scientific. However, by embracing materialism, the atheist has destroyed the possibility of knowledge, as well as science and technology. In other words, if atheism were true, it would be impossible to prove anything!

Here's why

Reasoning involves using the laws of logic. These include the law of non-contradiction which says that you can't have **A** and **not-A** at the same time and in the same relationship. For example, the statement "My car is in the parking lot, and it is not the case that my car is in the parking lot" is necessarily false by the law of non-contradiction. Any rational person would accept this law. But why is this law true? Why should there be a law of non-contradiction, or for that matter, any laws of reasoning? The Christian can answer this question. For the Christian there is an absolute standard for reasoning; we are to pattern our thoughts after God's. The laws of logic are a reflection of the way God thinks. The law of non-contradiction is not simply one person's opinion of how we ought to think, rather it stems from God's self-consistent nature. God cannot deny Himself (2 Timothy 2:13)[3], and so, the way God upholds the universe will necessarily be non-contradictory.

Laws of logic are God's standard for thinking. Since God is an unchanging, sovereign, immaterial Being, the laws of logic are abstract, universal, invariant entities. In other words, they are not made of matter—they apply everywhere and at all times. Laws of logic are contingent upon God's unchanging nature. And they are necessary for logical reasoning. Thus, rational reasoning would be impossible without the biblical God.

The materialistic atheist can't have laws of logic. He believes that everything that exists is material—part of the physical world. But laws of logic are not physical. You can't stub your toe on a law of logic. Laws of logic cannot exist in the atheist's world, yet he uses them to try to reason. This is inconsistent. He is borrowing from the Christian worldview to argue against the Christian worldview. The atheist's view cannot be rational because he uses things (laws of logic) that cannot exist according to his profession.

The debate over the existence of God is a bit like a debate over the existence of air.[3] Can you imagine someone arguing that air doesn't actually exist? He would offer seemingly excellent "proofs" against the existence of air, while simultaneously breathing air and expecting that we can hear his words as the sound is transmitted through the air. In order for us to hear and understand his claim, it would have to be wrong. Likewise, the atheist, in arguing that God does not exist must use laws of logic that only make sense if

God does exist. In order for his argument to make sense, it would have to be wrong.

How can the atheist respond?

The atheist might say, "Well, I can reason just fine, and I don't believe in God." But this is no different than the critic of air saying, "Well, I can breathe just fine, and I don't believe in air." This isn't a rational response. Breathing requires air, not a profession of belief in air. Likewise, logical reasoning requires God, not a profession of belief in Him. Of course the atheist can reason; it's because God has made his mind and given him access to the laws of logic—and that's the point. It's because God exists that reasoning is possible. The atheist can reason, but within his own worldview he cannot account for his ability to reason.

The atheist might respond, "Laws of logic are conventions made up by man." But conventions are (by definition) conventional. That is, we all agree to them and so they work—like driving on the right side of the road. But if laws of logic were conventional, then different cultures could adopt different laws of logic (like driving on the left side of the road). So, in some cultures it might be perfectly fine to contradict yourself. In some societies truth could be self-contradictory. Clearly that wouldn't do. If laws of logic are just conventions, then they are not universal laws. Rational debate would be impossible if laws of logic were conventional, because the two opponents could simply pick different standards for reasoning. Each would be right according to his own arbitrary standard.

The atheist might respond, "Laws of logic are material—they are made of electrochemical connections in the brain." But then the laws of logic are not universal; they would not extend beyond the brain. In other words, we couldn't argue that contradictions cannot occur on Mars, since no one's brain is on Mars. In fact, if the laws of logic are just electrochemical connections in the brain, then they would differ somewhat from person to person because everyone has different connections in their brain.

Sometimes an atheist will attempt to answer with a more pragmatic response: "We use the laws of logic because they work." Unfortunately for him, that isn't the question. We all agree the laws of logic work; they work because they're true. The question is why do they exist in the first place? How can the atheist account for absolute standards of reasoning like the laws of logic? How can non-material things like laws exist if the universe is material only?

As a last resort, the atheist may give up a strictly materialistic view and agree that there are immaterial, universal laws. This is a huge concession; after all, if a person is willing to concede that immaterial, universal, unchanging entities can exist, then he must consider the possibility that God exists. But this concession does not save the atheist's position. He must still justify the laws of logic. Why do they exist? And what is the point of contact between the material physical world and the immaterial world of logic? In other words, why does the material universe feel compelled to obey immaterial laws? The atheist cannot answer these questions. His worldview cannot be justified; it is arbitrary and thus irrational.

Objection: "The laws of logic (and causality, mathematics, etc.) are a necessary extension of the (macroscopic) laws of nature in this universe, and humankind has evolved enough to recognize and utilize these laws of logic".

Response: The argument is that laws of logic are a reflection of the thinking of the biblical God as revealed in the Scriptures, and that any alternative view really doesn't make sense. The hypothetical response that you have posed is essentially the conjecture that laws of logic are a reflection of the way the universe works. This position is also very easy to refute for a number of reasons.

First, it would be hard to support the notion that laws of logic are a reflection or extension of the physical universe because they do not describe the physical universe (as laws of nature do).

Rather, laws of logic pertain more to the reasoning process; they describe the correct "chain of reasoning" from premises to conclusions. For example, the law of non-contradiction (**A** and **not-A** cannot both be true at the same time and in the same relationship) deals with concepts—not with nature, per se. Laws of logic connect conceptual relationships, rather than describing specific conditions or processes in the physical universe.

More importantly, if laws of logic were a reflection of the universe (rather than of God's thoughts), then they would be contingent upon the universe. And that leads to some rather absurd consequences. If laws of logic were contingent on the universe, then we would expect that different parts of the universe would have different laws of logic. After all, the conditions in the core of the sun are quite different than conditions on the surface of earth. If laws of logic describe the universe, then they would be different from place to place, since different parts of the universe are described differently.

Moreover, if laws of logic were contingent upon the universe, then we would expect them to change with time, since the universe changes with time. Yet, we all presume that laws of logic are invariant—the same yesterday, today, and tomorrow. This, of course, makes sense in the Christian worldview, since God is beyond time, and, thus, His thoughts are as well. If laws of logic were merely an extension of the physical universe, then we would have no basis for arguing that they must apply in unknown regions of the universe or in the future, since no one has experienced these things. It does no good to counter that laws of logic do work in known regions and have always worked in the past. This is irrelevant to unknown regions and the future unless we already presupposed an underlying uniformity, which only the consistent Christian has a right to expect.

Mathematics is similar, reflecting the thinking of an infinite God. Mathematics is not an extension of the physical universe, even though natural laws can often be expressed in terms of mathematical principles. Mathematicians frequently entertain concepts that have no corresponding physical reality whatsoever. We could consider a 38-dimensional space and compute the hyper-volumes of hyper-spheres and other shapes in such mathematical realms. Such concepts would be perfectly meaningful, even though such things do not and cannot exist physically in our three-dimensional space.

By the way, laws of logic (and mathematics) are not violated even at the quantum scale or at relativistic velocities. Energy and mass are not contraries, and, so, there is no problem with an equivalence relationship. Even wave-particle duality is not truly contradictory; objects behave wavelike in some ways at some times, and particle-like at other times and in other ways. When the time or sense is different, there is no contradiction.

Objection: "One of the arguments went as, 'The uniformity of the universe is a property of the universe.' This is obviously an assumption as you also said. Why do we have to account for this uniformity?"

Response: The answer is this: in order to be rational. The mark of rationality is to have a good reason for what we believe. And remember, it is biblical to have a reason for what we believe (1 Peter 3:15). The two key forms of irrationality are inconsistency and arbitrariness (not having a reason). You can imagine that when an evolutionist asked why I believe in creation if I replied, "Oh, there's no reason—it's just true," then he would rightly point out that this is arbitrary and irrational. And yet, evolutionists do not have a good reason (on their own professed worldview) for their belief in uniformity—or for laws of logic. They are, therefore, being irrational. Biblical creation is the only rational position because it alone provides a reason for those things we take for granted—like uniformity and laws of logic.

It is fine to pose a hypothetical universe with stability and laws of logic. But those things would still need to be justified. How could we possibly know that the laws of logic are invariant (do not change with time), and not that they simply have not changed so far? And why does the material universe feel compelled to obey immaterial laws? How would we know that the laws are truly universal (applying everywhere) and invariant? The biblical creationist can answer these questions by pointing to God's special revelation, but these questions are simply not answerable apart from a biblical worldview. So, the evolutionist is still left without a good reason for why he believes in laws of logic, why they have the properties they do, and why the physical universe does not violate them. He is indeed "borrowing" from Christianity.

The Christian worldview is not a mere assumption. It is the worldview that makes knowledge possible (Proverbs 1:7; Colossians 2:3). It alone provides the justification for those things we need for reasoning—such as laws of logic and uniformity. And that is a pretty good reason to believe in Christianity. Even presuppositions require a reason; it's just that the reason is provided after the fact in the case of a presupposition. In summary, a good reason to believe in the Christian worldview is that without it, we couldn't reason at all.

Conclusions

Clearly, atheism is not a rational worldview. It is self-refuting because the atheist must first assume the opposite of what he is trying to prove in order to be able to prove anything. As Dr. Cornelius Van Til put it, "[A]theism presupposes theism." Laws of logic require the existence of God—and not just any god, but the Christian God. Only the God of the Bible can be the foundation for knowledge (Proverbs 1:7; Colossians 2:3).[4] Since the God of Scripture is immaterial, sovereign, and beyond time, it makes sense to have laws of logic that are immaterial, universal, and unchanging. Since God has revealed Himself to man, we are able to know and use logic. Since God made the universe and since God made our minds, it makes sense that our minds would have an ability to study and understand the universe. But if the brain is simply the result of mindless evolutionary processes that conveyed some sort of survival value in the past, why should we trust its conclusions? If the universe and our minds are simply the results of time and chance, as the atheist contends, why would we expect that the mind could make sense of the universe? How could science and technology be possible?

Rational thinking, science, and technology make sense in a Christian worldview. The Christian has a basis for these things; the atheist does not. This is not to say that atheists cannot be rational about some things. They can because they too are made in God's image and have access to God's laws of logic. But they have no rational basis for rationality within their own worldview. Likewise, atheists can be moral, but they have no basis for that morality according to what they claim to believe. An atheist is a walking bundle of contradictions. He reasons and does science, yet he denies the very God that makes reasoning and science possible. On the other hand, the Christian worldview is consistent and makes sense of human reasoning and experience.

---

1. "Atheists arise: Dawkins spreads the A-word among America's unbelievers," *The Guardian*, October 1st, 2007. www.theguardian.com/world/2007/oct/01/internationaleducationnews. religion.

2. Christian philosopher Dr. Greg Bahnsen often used this analogy. Dr. Bahnsen was known as the "man atheists most feared."

3. If we are faithless, He remains faithful; He cannot deny Himself (2 Timothy 2:13).

4. The fear of the LORD is the beginning of knowledge, but fools despise wisdom and instruction (Proverbs 1:7); in whom [Christ] are hidden all the treasures of wisdom and knowledge (Proverbs 1:7).

Jason Lisle, Director of Research, Institute for Creation Research

Dr. Lisle graduated *summa cum laude* from Ohio Wesleyan University where he double-majored in physics and astronomy and minored in mathematics. Jason earned a master's degree and a PhD in astrophysics at the University of Colorado.

Morality: The Secular Response

by Bodie Hodge

Morality has always been a problem for secular humanism and its various forms (e.g., atheism, agnosticism, naturalism, and the like).[1] In recent times some have tried to address this major problem, but their attempts fail miserably.

In a *New Scientist* article, there was a section conveying the latest secular thoughts on morality, as well as a brief article further in the magazine regarding the topic.[2] The section is titled, "If morality is broken, we can fix it."

That title caught my attention because there is no sure basis to say morality is broken outside of God and the absolute truth revealed in His Word. If one secularist says morality is broken and needs to be fixed, then another can say it is not broken and does not need to be fixed. So they are left with nothing but arbitrary opinions as people try to pick and choose their own morality.

Examining these secular claims

The article says, "Science has made great strides in explaining morality." This statement attributes human-like qualities to the methodology of "science," which is the fallacy of reification. "Science" does not explain things; *people* explain things. Sadly, this fallacy is made frequently on the secular side.

The article goes on to say, "No longer is [morality] seen as something handed down from on high ..." Though many secular humanists profess that morality is not set by God, the majority of people disagree and still recognize that morality does comes from

God. But does it really matter what people *think*, or is it about *what God says*?

The article continues, "… instead it is an evolved system of enlightened self-interest." If morality is really all about "self-interest," then who cares about the morality of others? Hitler was consumed with his own self-interest, and he was an evolutionist. So, was his morality acceptable by these evolutionary standards? I should hope not!

Next they say, "Altruism for example can benefit your genes and disgust can protect you from disease." What do they mean by "benefit"? Did you catch that? They are appealing to some overarching "good" in the universe by which to judge something as a "benefit." Secularists are borrowing from the biblical worldview when they propose that something such as a "benefit" or "good" exists. By so doing, they undercut the very argument they are trying to propose.

Furthermore, who are these people to say that "disgust" is a good thing or that being disease-free is a good thing? Such ideas are a reflection of Leviticus and the cleanliness laws from the Bible, which teaches to resist effects of a sin-cursed and broken world. But how can an evolutionist say that preventing disease is a good thing? Perhaps catching a disease and dying is what is needed for the next step of evolution.

Next, they comment that "this picture is progress, but it can also lead to a kind of fatalism, a belief that our moral values evolved for a good reason and so we should stick with them." So, now they are appealing to an overarching concept of "good" by which to judge these things? For people who claim that they no longer believe in morality being "handed down from on high," they have twice appealed to something higher that determines what is good and bad and governs everything. This is self-refuting!

In the article, the writer(s) further agreed that their moral guidelines are "arbitrary" and that "the rules are not set in stone," so there is nothing to stop them from getting rid of the rules they think don't work. I could continue, but I'm sure you understand the basics of how these arguments have failed.

This *New Scientist* article demonstrates that secular morality is baseless, and the writer(s) even appealed to Christian morality with an overarching "good" (probably without meaning to)—all the while saying morality is simply arbitrary and not based on an all-good God who declares what is right and wrong.

Conclusion

True morality from a secular perspective simply cannot exist—it is arbitrary and meaningless. Non-Christians have no choice but to borrow from a biblical worldview to make sense of morality—whether they realize it or not. In a way, I feel sorrow for those who have been secularized to believe morality is arbitrary; they don't know what they are missing when they fail to understand the truth.

From a biblical viewpoint, we have a basis for morality since we are made in the image of a perfectly moral Creator. Of course, there are still moral problems because we live in a world full of sin, thanks to our mutual grandfather Adam.

When you take God out of the equation, *everything* becomes arbitrary. Sadly, this is the world we live in, and the next generation of kids is being taught God doesn't exist and everything is subjective—not just morality, but even reality itself!

This is why the creation-gospel ministry of Answers in Genesis is so important in our modern age. Please stand with us as we battle for biblical authority against these false ideas that are permeating our culture. It is time to build your "house on the rock" of Jesus Christ instead of the false and sinking sand of secular ideas—especially when it comes to morality.

And this is the condemnation, that the light has come into the world, and men loved darkness rather than light, because their deeds were evil (John 3:19).

1. Humanism is the religion that essentially elevates man to the position of God to determine truth and likewise morality.

2. "If morality is broken, we can fix it," *New Scientist*, February 18, 2012, p. 3. Also in the same publication, Michael Marshal, "Moral choices show we are deeply split," p. 10. This second article points out that morality seems split on issues pertaining to ethical choices, but this should be expected when people are taught there is no absolute right and wrong. For those who did read this short article by Marshal, why did no volunteers offer to sacrifice themselves and be the one to jump off the train to save other people's lives? That is what our loving Creator did when He stepped into history to die in the place of mankind.

Bodie Hodge, speaker, writer, and researcher, Answers in Genesis

Bodie Hodge has a master's degree in mechanical engineering from Southern Illinois University at Carbondale. Since joining Answers in Genesis, Bodie has contributed to several books, including *Dragons: Legends and Lore of Dinosaurs.*

Self-refuting Skepticism

by Roger Patterson

Many people in modern society label themselves as skeptics. They publish magazines, participate in various organizations, raise funds to support their causes, and lobby the public through roadside signs, podcasts, and advertisements on buses.

Though there are several organizations to which we could refer, we will focus our attention on the Skeptics Society headed by Dr. Michael Shermer for sake of discussing the relevant points of agreement and disagreement. By explaining the positions given by this organization, you can easily apply them to others who share the same basic views. As Christians, we should have a biblically founded skepticism of the claims made by "skeptics" (Proverbs 18:17).

Skepticism is a humanistic philosophy. Humanists consider man to be the measure of all things. That is, the human mind is considered to be the ultimate standard by which all claims are judged. Humanism is a religious system, the deity of the worldview being man himself. Though the humanists would generally reject the label of religious, they certainly hold their views with zeal and conviction.

Another important element of the humanist religion is naturalism (or, materialism). This belief blindly asserts that nothing beyond nature exists; the physical universe is all that there is. Anything that is supernatural is excluded from this belief system. We will explain these two ideas as we look at the beliefs of skeptical humanists and their manifesto.

The following excerpts are taken from *A Skeptical Manifesto*, written by Dr. Michael Shermer, which will serve to illustrate the beliefs of those who claim to be skeptics.

To his credit, Dr. Shermer is openly honest about the failure of skepticism as a philosophy.

But what does it mean to be skeptical? Skepticism has a long historical tradition dating back to ancient Greece when Socrates observed: "All I know is that I know nothing." But this is not a practical position to take.

Shermer rightly concludes that if a skeptic were to apply his philosophy to his own views, he would have to be skeptical of skepticism—a position of absurdity. The very foundation of this belief system is self-refuting.

To avoid the absurdity of his argument, Shermer goes on to qualify his beliefs. He adds the qualifiers of rational and scientific to his belief system. He does this in order to justify his claim that he wishes to promote progress, even though skepticism itself does not hold that goal. Exactly what he means by progress is not explained, but it seems to tie into a later discussion of the evolution of mankind to higher levels. However, he provides no scientific or rational validation for what higher means and why his views should be accepted above other views of progress.

Scientific skepticism

Let us first look at the claim that skepticism must be scientific in order to be of value. Though not explicitly stated, the concept of materialism is present in the definition of science given by the Skeptics Society:

> . . . a set of mental and behavioral methods designed to describe and interpret observed or inferred phenomenon, past or present, aimed at building a testable body of knowledge open to rejection or confirmation.[1]

It is worth noting that this definition is simply given to persuade the reader to accept a particular view. It is not what would be found in textbooks and dictionaries. Redefining terms is simply a tactic of persuasion, not a logical argument.

Since his definition of science deals with observation, Shermer defines observation as "gathering data through the senses or sensory enhancing technologies." Although supernatural forces would not normally be experienced by the senses, the Christian rightly takes God to be the ultimate first cause of the things we do experience. This forces us to ask the question, "Why must supernatural explanations be removed from science?"

Dr. Shermer does not provide a reason for the assertion that science can only be based on observations by the senses. If this claim is left as an arbitrary assertion, then there is no logical reason to accept it. Christians should be skeptical of this skeptic's definition of science.

Another problem that this definition presents for the skeptics is that it is inconsistent. On the one hand, Shermer wants to include past events as falling under his definition of science. On the other hand, he wants to have observational confirmation or rejection of everything that is to be considered scientific knowledge. But, of course, past events are not subject to observational rejection or confirmation. Shermer tries to cover up this inconsistency by suggesting that inferences are as legitimate as observations, but provides no support for this view.

Shermer goes on to explain that most biologists would accept evolution as a "fact" in that it is based on "data or conclusions confirmed to such an extent it would be reasonable to offer temporary agreement." Since skeptical science can never ultimately prove anything, the temporary agreement of the community is that evolution happened and will continue to happen. This "fact" must be based on the inferences of past events from observations of things in the present, not observing and testing things from the past. Shermer argues from this "fact" at several points in this article.

Since facts, by definition, are true, this philosophy allows for the provisional acceptance of untrue facts. Many things that were once considered factual are known to be false today. In the absence of an absolute standard to determine truth, skeptics build their foundation on what they must admit could be false in the future—evolution included.

This naturalistic science is intended to be objective and avoid any mysticism. Creationism is said to "have been tested (and failed the tests) often enough that we can provisionally conclude [it is] false." If these tests were done according to the scientific method, it would interest us to know how the supernatural creation of the universe was observed through the senses (what measurements were involved) and shown to be false. The very claim is outside of the capabilities of the model of skeptical science set forward.

Rational skepticism

To prop up his self-refuting philosophy of skepticism, Dr. Shermer believes that there must be a rational component added so that the skeptic might think in a reliable way. He defines the rational skeptic as:

> One who questions the validity of particular claims of knowledge by employing or calling for statements of fact to prove or disprove claims, as a tool for understanding causality.

Since Dr. Shermer seems to be committed to a philosophy of naturalism, how does he account for the existence of reason? Reason involves using laws of logic—which are not part of nature. Laws of logic describe the correct chain of reasoning from premises to conclusions; they are not material and cannot exist in a materialistic universe. The naturalist cannot account for universal, invariant, abstract entities like laws of logic.

What the skeptic is doing is borrowing concepts from a biblical view of the universe while rejecting the system itself—an irrational approach. There is no explanation for the existence of reason and the laws of logic in a naturalistic worldview. If man is simply the accumulation of chemical reactions, why should we trust those reactions to understand the world around it? Chemical reactions and electrical impulses by themselves are neither right nor wrong; they simply are.

Science is only possible because God has ordered the universe and sustains it in such a way that the human mind can understand it. The Christian has an ultimate reason for believing that we can study and understand the universe. The naturalistic skeptic does not. (For a detailed explanation of this concept please see *Revelation, Speculation, and Science* by Dr. Greg Bahnsen.)

Dr. Shermer makes the claim that it would be unscientific to accept a dogmatic claim that is not based on scientific inquiry. But he expects us to accept his dogmatic assertion without proving it by any scientific means (which would be impossible). Again, an assertion is made with no rational reason to accept it.

Accepting ideas on the authority of another human can be dangerous; so, it is important to understand how the person making the claim came to know what is being claimed. We certainly don't disagree with Dr. Shermer on not accepting dogmatic claims, but it is ironic that he expects us to believe his claim without scientific proof. Christians should be skeptical of such claims.

There is, however, One whom we can trust absolutely. When He tells us of the world, we can accept those things, as He was not only an eyewitness, but the Creator of the universe. Having created the universe, we can trust that what God tells us about it through His Word can be taken as truth. Since there can be no higher authority than the Creator, we must accept His claims of truth over the claims made by fallible humans. God has granted us the gift of reason, humans having been created in His image, but we must recognize the limits of that reasoning and the condition of the fallen world in which we live.

Other skeptics have suggested that we cannot trust the Bible because it was written by men; of course, this statement itself was written by men. So, if that statement is trustworthy, that we cannot trust a statement written by men, then we cannot trust the statement itself about not trusting the Bible—a contradiction.

It is also worth noting that an argument really should be evaluated on its own merit, not on the source. To do otherwise is to commit the genetic fallacy. The Bible claims to be the Word of God, is internally consistent, and provides the only rational foundation for the world around us. On these grounds, not the empty claims of skeptical humans, we can accept the truth that God has revealed to us.

Conclusion

Mankind has elevated himself throughout history. From the Fall in the Garden, mankind has sought to be equal, if not superior, to God. Like any other philosophy that begins without God as the standard of truth, this humanistic philosophy is arbitrary and logically inconsistent. Applying a little biblically based skepticism to the claims of these skeptics exposes the flaws.

As we look to God's Word as the foundation for all thinking, we might also be moved to pray for those who suppress the truth of God in unrighteousness (Romans 1:18–19). Had God not revealed His truth to us, we would still be in that darkened condition (Ephesians 2:1–5). As we seek to share the truth with a lost world, let us remember to do so in meekness and fear and with thankfulness to God for the salvation He has granted us through Jesus Christ (1 Peter 3:15–16).

1.   www.skeptic.com/about_us/manifesto.html.

Roger Patterson, writer & editor, Answers in Genesis

Roger Patterson taught in public schools for eight years before joining Answers in Genesis. He earned his BS Ed degree in biology from Montana State University–Billings. Roger is the author of *Evolution Exposed* and serves on AiG's editorial review board.

Dear Atheists . . . Are You Tired of It All?

by Bodie Hodge

Are you tired of all the evil associated with the philosophy of atheism—Stalin, Hitler, Pol Pot, and so on?[1] After all, most murderers, tyrants, and rapists are not biblical Christians, and most have rejected the God of the Bible. Even if they claim to believe in the God of the Bible, they are not really living like a true Christ follower (who strives to follow God's Word), are they?

Do you feel conflicted about the fact that atheism has no basis in morality (i.e., no absolute right and wrong; no good, no bad?) If someone stabs you in the back, treats you like nothing, steals from you, or lies to you, it doesn't ultimately matter in an atheistic worldview where everything and everyone are just chemical reactions doing what chemicals do. And further, knowing that you are essentially no different from a cockroach in an atheistic worldview (since people are just animals) must be disheartening.

Are you tired of the fact that atheism (which is based in materialism,[2] a popular worldview today) has no basis for logic and reasoning? Is it tough trying to get up every day thinking that truth, which is immaterial, really doesn't exist? Are you bothered by the fact that atheism cannot account for uniformity in nature[3] (the basis by which we can do real science)? Why would everything explode from nothing and, by pure chance, form beautiful laws like $E=MC^2$ or $F=MA$?[4]

Do you feel like you need a weekend to recoup, even though a weekend is really meaningless in an atheistic worldview—since animals, like bees, don't take a day of rest or have a weekend? So why should atheists? Why borrow a workweek and weekend that comes from the pages of Scriptures, which are despised by atheists? Weeks and weekends come from God creating in six literal days and resting for a literal day; and then the Lord Jesus resurrected on the first day of the week (Sunday). And why look forward to time off for a holiday (i.e., holy day), when nothing is holy in an atheistic worldview?

For professing atheists, these questions can be overwhelming to make sense of within their worldview. And further, within an atheistic worldview, atheists must view themselves as God. Essentially, atheists are claiming to be God. Instead of saying there *may not* be a God, they say there is *no* God. To make such a statement, they must claim to be omniscient (which is an essential attribute of the God of the Bible) among other attributes of God as well.[5] So, by saying there is no God, the atheist refutes his own position by addressing the question as though he or she were God!

Do you feel conflicted about proselytizing the faith of atheism, since if atheism were true then who cares about proselytizing? Let's face it, life seems tough enough as an atheist without having to deal with other major concerns like not having a basis to wear clothes, or no basis for marriage, no consistent reason to be clean (snails don't wake up in the morning and clean themselves or follow other cleanliness guidelines based on Levitical laws), and no objective reason to believe in love.

Are you weary of looking for evidence that contradicts the Bible's account of creation and finding none?[6] Do the assumptions and inconsistencies of dating methods weigh on your conscience when they are misrepresented as fact?[7] Where do you suppose those missing links have gone into hiding? Surely the atheist sees the folly and hopelessness of believing that everything came from nothing.

In fact, why would an atheist care to live one moment longer in a broken universe where one is merely rearranged pond scum and all you have to look forward to is . . . death, which can be around any corner? And in 467 trillion years, no one will care one iota about what you did or who you were or how and when you died—because death is the ultimate "hero" in an atheistic, evolutionary worldview. Of course, as a Christian I disagree, and I have a basis to see you as having value.

Invitation

I invite you to reconsider that the false religion of atheism is simply that. I'm here to tell you that atheism is a lie (Romans 1:25).[8] As a Christian, I understand that truth exists because God exists, who is the Truth (John 14:6),[9] and we are made in His image.[10] Unlike an atheist, whose worldview doesn't allow him to believe in truth or lies, the Bible-believer has a foundation that enables him to speak about truth and lies. This is because believers in God and His Word have an authority, the ultimate authority on the subject, to base statements upon.

There is a God, and you are also made in His image (Genesis 1:26, 9:6).[11] This means you have value. Whereas consistent atheists teach that you have no value, I see you differently. I see you as a relative (Acts 17:26)[12] and one who—unlike animals, plants, and fallen angels—has the possibility of salvation from death, which is the result of sin (i.e., disobedience to God; see Romans 6:23).[13] We have all fallen short of God's holy standard of perfect obedience thanks to our mutual grandfather, Adam (Romans 5:12).[14] And God sees you differently, too (John 3:16).[15] While you were still a sinner, God stepped into history to become a man to die in your place (Romans 5:8)[16] and offer the free gift of salvation (Ephesians 2:8–9).[17]

Atheists have no consistent reason to proselytize their faith, but Christians like me do have a reason—Jesus Christ, who is the Truth, commands us to (Matthew 28:19).[18] We want to see people repent of their evil deeds and be saved from death (Acts 8:22, 17:30).[19] What a wonderful joy (Luke 15:10)[20].

Where atheists have no basis for logic and reason (or even for truth, since truth is immaterial), Bible believers can understand that mankind is made in the image of a logical and reasoning God who is the truth. Hence, Christians can make sense of things because in Christ are "hidden all the treasures of wisdom and knowledge" (Colossians 2:3).[21] Christians also have a basis to explain why people sometimes don't think logically due to the Fall of mankind in Genesis 3. The most logical response is to give up atheism and receive Jesus Christ as Lord and Savior to rescue you from sin and death (Romans 10:13).[22] Instead of death, God promises believers eternal life (1 John 2:25; John 10:28)[23] and in 467 trillion years, you will still have value in contrast to the secular view of nothingness.

Christians do have a basis to wear clothes (to cover shame due to sin; see Genesis 2:25, 3:7),[24] a reason to uphold marriage (God made a man and a woman; see Genesis 1:27; Matthew 19:4–6),[25] a reason to be clean (Leviticus contains many provisions to counter diseases in a sin-cursed world), and a source of real love (since God made us in His loving image; see 1 John 4:8).[26] As Christians, we have a solid foundation for saying things like back-stabbing, theft, and lies are wrong (see the Ten Commandments in Exodus 20).

I invite you to leave the false religion of atheism and its various forms and return to the one true God who came to rescue you (John 17:3).[27] Jesus Christ, who is God the Son, loved you enough to come down and die in our place so we can experience God's goodness for all eternity instead of the wrath of God for all eternity in hell (Matthew 25:46).[28] And we all have sentenced ourselves to judgment because of our disobedience to God and rejection of Him (John 3:17–18).[29]

The day is coming when we all will give an account before God for our actions and thoughts (Romans 14:12).[30] Will you repent and receive Christ as your Lord and Savior today so that you will join Christ in the resurrection from the dead (John 11:25;

Romans 6:5)?[31] I invite you personally to become an ex-atheist, join the ranks of the saved through Jesus Christ, and become a new creation (2 Corinthians 5:17)[32] as we continue to advance with the gospel in peace that only God can provide (Romans 5:1).[33]

---

1. See "Evolutionary Humanism: The Bloodiest Religion Ever" in this book on p. 19.

2. See "Atheism: An Irrational Worldview" in this book on p. 51.

3. J. Lisle, "Evolution: The Anti-science," Answers in Genesis, February 13, 2008, www. answersingenesis.org/articles/aid/v3/n1/evolution-anti-science.

4. K. Ham, Gen. Ed., New Answers Book 1, Lisle, J., "Don't creationists deny the laws of nature?" Master Books, Green Forest AR, 2006, pp. 39–46, www.answersingenesis.org/articles/nab/creationists-deny-laws-of-nature.

5. If one claims that God may exist or that there may be a spiritual realm, then that person is not an atheist, but an agnostic, at best. The agnostic says that one cannot know whether God exists, but how can they know that for certain apart from being omniscient themselves? Additionally, the Bible says in 1 John 5:13 that we can know for certain that we have eternal life. So an agnostic—who claims we cannot know—does not hold a neutral position regarding the biblical God.

6. K. Ham, "Missing? or Misinterpreted?" Answers in Genesis, March 1, 2004, www.answersingenesic.org/articles/cm/v26/n2/missing.

7. K. Ham, New Answers Book 1, M. Riddle, "Does radiometric dating prove the earth is old?" Master Books, Green Forest, AR, 2006, pp. 113–134, www.answersingenesis.org/articles/nab/does-radiometric-dating-prove.

8. Who exchanged the truth of God for the lie, and worshiped and served the creature rather than the Creator, who is blessed forever. Amen (Romans 1:25).

9. Jesus said to him, "I am the way, the truth, and the life. No one comes to the Father except through Me" (John 14:6).

10. Keep in mind that Christians, including me, do fall short due to sin and the Curse, but God never fails.

11. Then God said, "Let Us make man in Our image, according to Our likeness; let them have dominion over the fish of the sea, over the birds of the air, and over the cattle, over all the earth and over every creeping thing that creeps on the earth" (Genesis 1:26); Whoever sheds man's blood, by man his blood shall be shed; for in the image of God He made man (Genesis 9:6).

12. And He has made from one blood every nation of men to dwell on all the face of the earth, and has determined their preappointed times and the boundaries of their dwellings (Acts 17:26).

13. For the wages of sin is death, but the gift of God is eternal life in Christ Jesus our Lord (Romans 6:23).

14. Therefore, just as through one man sin entered the world, and death through sin, and thus death spread to all men, because all sinned (Romans 5:12).

15. For God so loved the world that He gave His only begotten Son, that whoever believes in Him should not perish but have everlasting life (John 3:16).

16. But God demonstrates His own love toward us, in that while we were still sinners, Christ died for us (Romans 5:8).

---

17. For by grace you have been saved through faith, and that not of yourselves; it is the gift of God, not of works, lest anyone should boast (Ephesians 2:8–9).

18. Go therefore and make disciples of all the nations, baptizing them in the name of the Father and of the Son and of the Holy Spirit (Matthew 28:19).

19. Repent therefore of this your wickedness, and pray God if perhaps the thought of your heart may be forgiven you (Acts 8:22); Truly, these times of ignorance God overlooked, but now commands all men everywhere to repent (Acts 17:30).

20. Likewise, I say to you, there is joy in the presence of the angels of God over one sinner who repents (Luke 15:10).

21. In whom [Christ] are hidden all the treasures of wisdom and knowledge (Colossians 2:3).

22. For 'whoever calls on the name of the Lord shall be saved' (Romans 10:13).

23. And this is the promise that He has promised us—eternal life (1 John 2:25);
And I give them eternal life, and they shall never perish; neither shall anyone snatch them out of My hand (John 10:28).

24. And they were both naked, the man and his wife, and were not ashamed (Genesis 2:25);
Then the eyes of both of them were opened, and they knew that they were naked; and they sewed fig leaves together and made themselves coverings (Genesis 3:7).

25. So God created man in His own image; in the image of God He created him; male and female He created them (Genesis 1:27); And He answered and said to them, "Have you not read that He who made them at the beginning 'made them male and female,' and said, 'for this reason a man shall leave his father and mother and be joined to his wife, and the two shall become one flesh'? So then, they are no longer two but one flesh. Therefore what God has joined together, let not man separate" (Matthew 19:4–6).

26. He who does not love does not know God, for God is love (1 John 4:8).

27. And this is eternal life, that they may know You, the only true God, and Jesus Christ whom You have sent (John 17:3).

28. And these will go away into everlasting punishment, but the righteous into eternal life (Matthew 25:46).

29. For God did not send His Son into the world to condemn the world, but that the world through Him might be saved. He who believes in Him is not condemned; but he who does not believe is condemned already, because he has not believed in the name of the only begotten Son of God (John 3:17–18).

30. So then each of us shall give account of himself to God (Romans 14:12).

31. Jesus said to her, "I am the resurrection and the life. He who believes in Me, though he may die, he shall live" (John 11:25); For if we have been united together in the likeness of His death, certainly we also shall be in the likeness of His resurrection. (Romans 6:5).

32. Therefore, if anyone is in Christ, he is a new creation; old things have passed away; behold, all things have become new (2 Corinthians 5:17).

33. Therefore, having been justified by faith, we have peace with God through our Lord Jesus Christ (Romans 5:1).

Confessions of a Former Atheist

by John UpChurch

My story starts in a small college town. We had moved there a few years before as an escape for my father, a former pastor who had given up on a church that had given up on him.

I would not say that my father was an openly religious man (even during his years as a minister), and he had never told us what to believe. When we had moved there, he became even more reticent. The only conversations that I remember having with him about his faith concerned the "fluidity" of biblical interpretation—something he had learned from seminary. To be honest, looking back, I am not sure he ever believed what he had once preached. Being the son of a minister, despite certain expectations, does not mean that you will have any sort of faith in God.

To be fair, I did try it. My mother has never given up on her belief, and she made sure that we at least went to church occasionally. It was a timid experiment to say the least: four boys who preferred high jinx to hymns. But we enjoyed our church bulletin artwork and crawling under the pews whenever the chance arose. We were mostly biding our time until we turned 16 and could make the "adult" decision not to go to church. It turned out, however, that we really didn't have to wait that long.

The older we got, the more my parents drifted apart. My mom occasionally made the sojourn to church, often carting me along as the youngest. I went because I had some friends who went; I went because I thought it was good to do so. But I did not see church as anything more than a location with other people.

As any child of the 1980s, I spent much of my youth getting information from educational programs on cable and PBS. I was voracious to learn everything I could about the world, about the universe, about matter, space, time. I wanted to learn it all, and there never seemed to be enough resources. In those dark ages before the Internet, there were only so many books at our library and only so many TV shows. I absorbed everything I could about dinosaurs and our "ancient" cosmos and the history of the earth. In fact, I spent my summer vacations reading in my room.

I have to admit that I was marginally interested in religion in general during that time, and I studied ancient mythology. But I found the Bible itself to be rather dry. *Thees* and *Thous* were not nearly as interesting to me as star formation, animal habitats, and chemical processes. That, I believed, was where the "good stuff" was.

What I did study of the Bible led more to questions than answers. On one hand, I was reading a paleontology book that could lay out a timeline of dinosaurs and their extinction. On the other hand, I didn't see anything about them in the Bible.[1] If God were truly God, surely He would have to have said something. But my footnotes were stubbornly silent (though I do recall them mentioning something about a hippo or elephant in Job).

When I think back, I lost all confidence in the Bible at a youth group meeting during high school. The main pastor of our large church met with us to answer some of our most serious questions about God, the Bible, life, and anything else. We all took a scrap piece of paper, wrote our question on it, and placed it in a hat. Many of the questions, given that we were teenage boys, had to do with relationships and girls, but my question was very different and simple: where are dinosaurs in the Bible? He purposefully skipped my question.

Really, I didn't want an answer. My father's "fluidity" lessons had taught me that there was no reason to trust what the Bible said. And the fruit of saying that the Bible (especially the first few books) is full of mythological stories and allegories was that I had no reason to believe that any of it was true. If the Bible wasn't true for history or science, then there was no reason to trust it for spiritual purposes: if the Bible can't be trusted on what people can see, it is very unlikely that they will trust it on what they can't see.

When the pastor skipped my question, I decided that the books and TV programs had better answers. It was just that simple.

A course in college

I had decided to be an anthropologist—or astronomer—or philosopher—or poet—or teacher. College, after all, was a cornucopia of options, and I loved the freedom of it all. My advisors didn't understand my good grades coupled with my "extended stay." I had convinced myself that they just didn't understand my desire to take it all in, be everything all at once.

I was free; I was miserable. My parents were continuing to drift apart, and I felt like my life was quickly spiraling down. I convinced myself that all the anger and sadness in my life would make excellent writing material, since that's all that I had. There is, after all, no hope when you believe that you are nothing more than a collection of senseless electrons, winding down— when you believe that your life is merely the end result of millions of random genetic mistakes.

But I could argue against the existence of God with the best of my peers. In fact, it was about that time that I was introduced to something amazingly ridiculous by an anthropology professor. Before then, I had never really thought it conceivable that someone would take the Bible literally or think that the earth was young. When I think back, I find it ironic that except for an atheist professor, I may never have even heard of young-earth creation. However, at the time, I howled in delight as she explained how some Christians believed that men had one less rib because God took one to make Eve. I also secretly derided one of her religious friends that she told us about who found no disunity between evolution and the Bible. That person, I decided, was simply someone who could not give up on an archaic belief system and was clinging to a "crutch."

On the other hand, I was interested in knowing how someone could ever believe that the earth was 6,000 years old. In several of my classes, I later heard about Archbishop Ussher's calculation for the age of the earth, and I decided to look it up at some point when I needed a good laugh.

Something from nothing

My parents separated in 2003, and I was never the same again. I slid into severe depression with suicidal tendencies and sought help at the university's therapy center. After two months, the sessions ended, but my depression did not—nor my thoughts and plans for suicide. By March of that year, I had my strategy laid out and my note written. I did not believe in heaven or hell, and I certainly did not believe that I was accountable to anyone or anything. My life was mine alone.

I didn't go through with my suicide attempt because of a single phrase. At the moment I had planned to finish the job, one simple phrase came to my mind, one solitary verse: "In the beginning was the Word, and the Word was with God, and the Word was God." I did not know what the phrase meant, nor did I know where it came from. But given my voracity to know as much as possible, it was enough to keep me from following through. However, it wasn't until a few months later that I even tried to figure it out.

The first one

After this, I received my BA in English, and I took a job in information technology. The job was, in many ways, a less-than-stressful occupation, and most of my time was spent setting up computers and monitoring the nightly backup of a server. This did allow a great deal of time to read the news on the Internet while I waited for the system to finish recording.

It was during this time that I met my first living, breathing, walking, talking young-earth creationist. I did not know he was a creationist for several weeks, but he and I spent a great deal of time talking about my family and the recent issue with my parents. But when I did find out, I have to admit that I felt like I was studying an undiscovered species—a living fossil, per se. He believed, and I felt like I should get a scalpel to examine his brain. Although my first instinct was to beat him over the head with the "facts" of the age of the earth and evolution, I decided instead to let him talk.

And what surprised me is that, first of all, he didn't believe that men have one less rib—I assumed he must simply have missed that part of his Sunday school lesson. He also was very rational in the reasons why he believed. As per my training, I figured he was "cherry-picking" the data he used to counter evolutionary claims. The mantra I was taught and clung to was that the wealth of evidence and all credible scientists supported billions of years. Case closed.

Waiting for backup

After a few weeks, I finally agreed to go to a website that my creationist friend had told me about: www.answersingenesis.org. Why did I go? Was I searching for the truth? Sadly, I went to the site because I wanted to see what ridiculous claims these people were making. It had been a rough day, and comedy was in order. And I laughed—hard—that first night. I laughed so much, in fact, that I went back the next night and the night after that. I found Ussher, and I found people with doctorates who actually believed that the earth was 6,000 years old. I also found a good number of evolutionary sites that laughed with me over that first week.

But I also found something else. There, buried in the archives, was an interesting story about the peppered moths[2] that I had studied throughout my childhood. There was some question as to the validity of these experiments that were put forth as one of the cornerstones of evolutionary thought. I didn't believe it at first, but I found correlating evidence on other secular sites as well. That may not seem like much to many people, but it caused a subtle shift in my thinking. And then there was the Miller-Urey experiment: classic foundational truth of abiogenesis. But why had no one ever bothered to discuss chirality? Why was that left out? Sure, I could find sites all over the Internet that attempted to address these issues and how they didn't disprove evolution, but what I was concerned with was the fact that they had never been brought up before. It was as if all the difficult spots in evolutionary theory had been whitewashed.

The only controversy I had ever been taught concerning the history of the world was *where* life had originated and *how* it developed from there. I had never even thought to question the foundational principles; I had never even considered taking a metaphysical look at the framework that I assumed to be truth. The unspoken rule seemed to be that anyone who did would automatically become contemptible. One could be a genius one moment (as long as they followed the evolutionary principles) and an idiot as soon as one stepped beyond those bounds.

Now, I wanted to know why I based all my preconceptions on an evolutionary foundation. It wasn't so much that I believed the creationist material; it was just that I needed to start with "what did I know" and "how did I know it." I began re-reading some of my anthropology textbooks with an eye to find the basis for the extrapolations. What I found was that the texts themselves assumed evolution to be true from the beginning. Thus, all data was interpreted to fit that paradigm. Many of my professors had often accused creationists of the same thing as a means to destroy their arguments. But these textbooks, too, were starting from a framework (naturalism) to construct hypotheses.

To be honest, the one recurring argument I read on the Internet to support evolution was the same "all evidence supports it" argument. But I found that to be very unsatisfying. Where was all this evidence? All dating methods have to assume certain conditions in order to work. Fossils also have to be interpreted. Though I continued to read the rebuttal sites, their arguments were increasingly unsatisfying, and all of them continued to pound the "all evidence, all scientists." This is characteristic, I found, of a great deal of anti-creationist literature—not suffocating, scintillating proofs of evolution, but, rather, angry attacks on scientific credentials, intellect, and sanity, caricatures, even hopes of "removal" through natural (and not-so-natural) selection. When I wanted proof, the only thing I found was vitriol.

I did not realize how much of an impact these discoveries were having on me until I began disagreeing with TV shows and books that I had previously accepted without question. It was also about this time that I discovered *Evidence that Demands a Verdict* by Josh McDowell (a former agnostic)—a book that completely transformed what I thought I "knew" about the unreliability of the Bible, a book that made me want to try reading that dusty tome once again.

And when I picked up the Bible, not knowing where to start, I decided that John would be a good place (the name of that book is fairly catchy, after all). There, on the first page and the first line, I read that same verse that had stayed my hand so many months before, even though I had not read it in many years: "In the beginning was the Word, and the Word was with God, and the Word was God"—in the beginning, indeed. Those words became my prayer of confession and obeisance that day and everyday since.

A glance back

Since coming to know the Lord, it has never ceased to amaze me when pastors say that accepting a literal Genesis has nothing to do with salvation. After all, they say, people have interpreted Genesis differently throughout history. But I rejected the gospel message for most of my life for the very reason that these pastors say doesn't matter. If secular science trumps Genesis, then it trumps Christ's message of salvation, too.

To those pastors, I ask, "If not on Genesis, where will you stand? Why should the world listen to the message of redemption when the very people who are preaching it don't believe what God says?" This is not a back-burner issue; this is not something secondary. I am living proof that people need answers, and if they don't get them at church, they *will* find them somewhere else.

---

1. Turns out I wasn't looking for the right things when trying to find dinosaurs in the Bible. See "You don't 'fit' dinosaurs with the Bible!" (www.answersingenesis.org/articles/2000/04/14/dont-fit-dinosaurs).

2. This article is an update to the article I originally read. Recent findings have upheld the data of the original study, but the methodology called the whole experiment into question. That said, there is no disconcerting data for creationists in any of the studies, for what was found was merely natural selection, which creationists don't conflate with molecules-to-man evolution, as evolutionists tend to.

John UpChurch, Senior Editor of BibleStudyTools.com and Jesus.org

John UpChurch serves as the editor for Jesus.org and is a contributor to the Answers in Genesis website. He graduated *summa cum laude* from the University of Tennessee with a BA in English.

"There Is No God!"

The Bible clearly says, "There is no God." Really. But the context is important.

The fool has said in his heart, "There is no God."
They are corrupt,
They have done abominable works,
There is none who does good.
The LORD looks down from heaven upon the children of men,
To see if there are any who understand, who seek God.
They have all turned aside,
They have together become corrupt;
There is none who does good,
No, not one. (Psalm 14:1–3)

God calls those who reject His existence fools not because they are stupid, but because they willingly reject what they know to be true. The ordered complexity that is present in the universe leaves everyone who looks at the world around them—especially in this age of scientific knowledge—without excuse. They know there is a God, and they know He is powerful, but they suppress that truth in unrighteousness to serve their own desires rather than the Creator (Romans 1:18–32).

Is that true of you? Do you recognize the attributes of God present in the spiral of a sunflower or the beauty and immensity of a galaxy, and yet you have a desire to run away from the Creator of those things?

When God created the universe, He created a world that was "very good." The first man and woman lived in perfect harmony with God. But that perfect relationship was broken when they rebelled against their Creator by disobeying His command. At that point, the relationship between God and man was broken. That broken relationship has been passed to every descendant of Adam and Eve, including you, as original sin. That sin has corrupted the entire earth and even the hearts and minds of people.

What is your attitude toward God? Even if you are suppressing the truth of His existence, the Bible makes it clear that you are impacted by original sin. This is evident in your actions and thoughts. When asked about the greatest commandment given by God to man, Jesus responded with a summary of the first four of the ten Commandments: You shall love the Lord your God with all your heart, with all your soul, and with all your mind (Matthew 22:34–40; Deuteronomy 6:5).

Can you say that you desire to love God with all of your heart, soul, and mind? Can you say that you desire to follow God's commands found in the Bible? If not, then the rebellion that was in Adam's heart is also in your heart. And because God is a just judge, He must punish those who rebel against Him. As the Creator, God has the right to establish the rules for His creation and to judge those who rebel. That is the bad news of sin in the world. That bad news means that you are separated as a rebel against your Creator.

But God made a way for the bad news to be turned to good news! God stepped into the world when Jesus was born to a virgin. Jesus, the God-man, lived a perfect life and perfectly obeyed every command of God in thought, word, and deed. He then went willingly to the Cross to be crucified and to take the punishment for sin upon Himself. He acted as a substitute, taking the punishment we deserve, and He offers us His righteousness.

Anyone who turns from his or her sins and submits to Jesus as Lord, trusting in His life, death, and Resurrection as the basis of being reconciled to God, will be forgiven and seen as righteous before God.

Humble yourself and submit to Jesus as both your Creator and Savior.

> But God has chosen the foolish things of the world to put to shame the wise, and God has chosen the weak things of the world to put to shame the things which are mighty; and the base things of the world and the things which are despised God has chosen, and the things which are not, to bring to nothing the things that are, that no flesh should glory in His presence. But of Him you are in Christ Jesus, who became for us wisdom from God—and righteousness and sanctification and redemption—that, as it is written, "He who glories, let him glory in the Lord" (1 Corinthians 1:27–31).